Epic Good News

A Poem of Our Divine Universe

Nelson P. Miller

Epic good news—a poem of our divine universe.

Miller, Nelson P.

Published by:

Crown Management LLC – January 2019

1527 Pineridge Drive
Grand Haven, MI 49417
USA

ISBN-13: 978-1-7322387-9-4

For my beloved Spirit, dearest friend,
And those who listen to him to obey.

Contents

Foreword

This epic poem in blank verse (iambic pentameter) follows the acts of the Messiah Jesus Christ, from creation to incarnation, baptism, ministry, crucifixion, resurrection, and soon-coming return. The poem's outline of the Rescuer's greatest-ever story is from a book-length New Testament study *Spiritspeak: Sharing Some Very Good News.* I wrote *Spiritspeak* in entirely non-religious language to support readers who are unfamiliar with or resistant to biblical terms and forms. *Spiritspeak* used no religious terms like God, Christ, Messiah, and resurrection, nor did it use familiar character names like Nicodemus, Herod, Pontius Pilate, Felix, and Gamaliel, or place names like Jerusalem, Samaria, the Gadarenes, and Rome. While *Spiritspeak* may in that form serve its conceived purpose, my deliberate omission of so many treasured Bible reference points, both religious terms and Bible names and places, serves poorly the well-versed Bible reader.

This epic poem remedies that omission for its different Bible-versed audience. Indeed, not only does the poem use New Testament names and places, it also draws heavily on Old Testament references. Because some or many of those references may be obscure even to the inveterate Bible reader, the poem includes in subscript text the Bible's referenced book, chapter, and verse, using abbreviations for which the book supplies an appendix. (Many citations intend to refer to a passage rather than just a verse, although citing just the first verse of the passage.) I hope that those references aid rather than distract you, encouraging you to explore once again the many rich stories that the Bible embeds in the Rescuer's greatest-ever New Testament story. For some readers, recognizing or guessing at the many references may be the reading's greatest fun. Christ embodies the Old Testament's glory.

Why blank verse in its iambic-pentameter form? John Milton wrote *Paradise Lost*, the English language's greatest epic poem, in blank verse. Vanity aside, I make no pretense of writing with anything approaching Milton's extraordinary skill. He will always remain for me a great literary and considerable spiritual hero. Yet admirers may prove their devotion even by poor imitation. More so, this poem may honor my beloved friend Holy Spirit whose voice I seek deep in the Bible's pages. The iambic-pentameter constraints of blank verse force reader and writer to consider the poem's words carefully, while simultaneously encouraging creative use of name-and-place references. Blank verse's constraint is also its liberty, much like the Spirit sets us free by aiding our submission to the Father, relying on the Son's one great work. Enjoy, and listen for the Spirit.

Book 1: Creation

Beginning

Embrace extraordin'ry ancient truth:

    Rapt love between divine Father and Son,

Like 'tween David and Saul's son Jonathan,*1 Sam 20:18*

    Least-apostle Paul and God-son Timothy,*1 Cor 4:17*

Boaz and Ruth, Elijah and 'Lisha,

    Grounds all reason, alone, for existence.

Though Adam's Eve eats prodigal's leaves,*Gen 3:6*

    Man doth not soil God's outpouring ov'rflow.

Spoken into being,*Ro 4:17* Father through Son Word,*Jn 1:1*

    Creation came, Son initiating,*Col 1:18*

He who with Father has no beginning,*Heb 7:3*

    Like high-priest Melchiz'dek, nor end of life,*Gen 14:18*

That how created would join Creators,*Jn 16:33*

    All could assume the Father's innocence,*Ro 2:5*

Follow the Father's Spirit, not world's way,*1Co 2:12*

    Nor waging world's wars,*2Co 10:3* but siblings of Son,*Jn 16:8*

Who seated athrone restores, all renews,*Rev 21:5*

    That to honor Father, love would defeat death,

This victory won not by hard war waged

But by hard submission Son painful made.

Father's word created kingdom and earth,

His paradise, yours Adam's twisted birth,*2Pe 3:5*

Father sharing heaven's hints and glimmers,*Jas 1:17*

Too, celestial beings like flames of fire,*Heb 1:7*

Spirit sharing secrets would angels rapt,*1Pe 1:12*

Kingdom res'dents bearing his name alone.*Eph 3:14*

So set your mind on Father's things above,*Col 3:2*

Looking down on none, as God advocates,*Matt 18:10*

Like children all pursuing only Son,

Need only of which we reach our Father.*Matt 19:13*

Purpose

Creation took not just form but purpose,

Made of Father to honor only Son,*Jn 17:4*

Father orig'nated through and for Son,*Col 1:16*

His invisible Father's own image,*Col 1:15*

Cause and consequence, creation made, as

Abra'm offered Isaac on Moriah,*Gen 22:9*

Elkanah and Hannah gave Samuel,*1 Sam 1:23*

Mordecai moved Esther, each to purpose,*1 Sam 20:18*

Son radiates his Father's one purpose,*Heb 1:3*

Son living deity loving Father*Col 2:9*

Above all else, one true source, for your sake.*1 Pe 1:20*

Perfect and forever, as you will be,*Heb 7:28*

If only you enter Father's one realm

Rather than remain corrupted of world,*Col 2:20*

Soulish stuff tethering heart to dead earth,

Violating no-idol commandment first,_Lev 26:1_

Cutting and burning wood to warm yourself

　　While worshipping a god carved from same wood,_Isa 44:15_

Warming you and baking your bread, but then

　　You pray to the same wood: save me! Save me!_Isa 44:16_

For what value is a craftsman's idol,

　　But a worthless image that teaches lies?_Hab 2:18_

And like Achan's sin, taking as plunder

　　Defeated people's devoted things,_Joshua 7:1_

Stoned dead for violating Lord's command,_Joshua 7:25_

　　When obeying, Lord's blessing should pursue,

Not for bigger barns to store but for love,_Luke 12:18_

　　Willing rather to treat all as God's own,

As David fin'lly slept in God's purpose,

　　Buried with ancestors, body decayed,_Acts 13:36_

But soul at rest in Abraham's bosom,_Luke 16:22_

　　To wait for salvation's grace-filled echo.

Participation

Yet Son did not then relinquish roy'l charge,

　　But instead partic'pates, holds all t'gether,_Col 1:17_

Spoken word sustaining everything,_Heb 1:3_

　　The world ripe with his thought, Son glory wrought,

His perfect light turn orb's axis aright,

　　Director entering his own filmed work,

Mary born and Joseph safely cradled,_Luke 2:7_

　　As Levite woman Moses papyrus

Bore, royal through hands of Pharaoh's daughter,_Ex 2:3_

To free chosen nation, called to free all.

Then rested the perfect Trinity Being,*Gen 2:2*

    Man now made in storied, gloried image,

Woman Eve yet to rise, Adam's rib borne,*Gen 2:21*

    Tender helper friend, painful bearer, too,

In flesh alone of future human race,

    Spirit supplied of Father God, who then

Rested that you remember his Word's work,*Heb 4:4*

    You also to welcome Sabbath rest,*Heb 4:9* though

Inner and outer rest world offers not,*Heb 4:10*

    But gentle Son rejoices to give you,*Matt 11:28*

As Jacob rested and worshipped on staff,*Gen 47:31*

    No builder of Lord's house laboring vain,*Psalm 127:1*

Spending strength for naught with all in Lord's hand,*Isaiah 49:4*

    Rather welcome love of One who rest is.*1John 4:8*

Perfection

You also know the Father's direction,

    Forward and up toward his perfection;

You feel this sense of liberty waiting,*Ro 8:19*

    This wonder as children of creation,*Ro 8:21*

Made so much more wonder that he decides

    Who honor wins,*Ro 8:33* not arbitrary choice

But freely on Son rely, him rescued,*Ro 8:24*

    Blood-cleansed of death,*Col 1:22* by Spirit guaranteed,*Eph 1:13*

Converted dead to living, done to begun,*Gal 3:14*

    Spirit sealed for your eternal return,*Eph 4:30*

Josiah-like, eye sound, not left or right,*2Kings 22:2*

Asa-like, too, righteous in the Lord's eyes,*1Kings 15:11*

Joash,*2Kings 12:2* Amazziah,*2Kings 15:3* Uzziah,*2Kings 15:34* kings

All, hearing Spirit groan for Son's rescue.*Ro 8:22*

Father blew his Spirit breath into man,*Gen 2:7*

Making man not just material but more,*Ro 9:21*

Spiritual, to enjoy his kingdom realm,

Imbued with his beauty as evidence,*Ecc 3:11*

Ruled not self but for good in wicked world,*Matt 13:24*

As lawless men pursue things, God bereft.*Matt 13:36*

For Father did not hell create for man

But man's enemy and devil legions,*Ro 25:41*

Body-burning refuse-dump Gehenna,*Mark 9:47*

Where false priests burned their own children alive,*Jer 7:31*

Fair to occupy their own hell torment,*Luke 16:25*

Fire unquenched by dipped fingertip to tongue.*Luke 16:24*

'Stead, Son prepared heaven for you as home,*John 14:2*

Paradise regained when all man had lost,*Luke 23:43*

And gained purely grace by confession 'lone,*Luke 23:42*

Whether 'fessed early or latest of late,*Matt 20:1*

Perfection come only under Father,

When Father and Son all ever do rule.

Demonstration

But God did not mere declare himself true,

Yet demonstrated utter love for you,*Matt 20:1*

From shepherds' first announcement that heaven

Itself rejoiced with Son come in rescue,*Luke 2:13*

All God's angels at Father's command to

7

Worship his Son so superior to them,*Heb 1:6*

As first demonstration of all men come,

    Remade of One's spiritual paradise.*1Co 15:47*

God showed his power in many times past,

    Ten mir'cles rebuking Egypt's Pharaoh,*Exo 13:15*

Until freedom his hand won, hard pursued,

    Waters moment parted again inundate,*Exo 15:19*

Elijah's consuming Carmel-top fire,*1Kings 18:19*

    Raining down from heaven at humble prayer,*1Kings 18:38*

Later chariots to carry him 'loft,*2Kings 2:12*

    Servant Elisha then greater mir'cles

Perform, such ax head float,*2Kings 6:6* oil overflow,*2Kings 4:5*

    And Shunammite's son restore to life,*2Kings 4:35*

Among battles won without lifted hand,

    Blinding enemy army on with word,*2Kings 6:18*

Jericho's walls falling to trumpet blare,*Joshua 6:20*

    War's sun standing still at Joshua's request,*Joshua 10:13*

Aaron and Hur upholding Moses' arms,*Exo 17:12*

    Lord's army marching in David's tree tops,*2Sam 5:24*

Hundred eighty-five thousand Assyr'ans

    Angel-army subdued in night attack.*2Kings 19:35*

Son showed gentler hue, though followers dread,

    Walking on waves of water as were ghost,*Matt 14:26*

Gentler still when wine of wedding water,*John 2:1*

    And provident with astonishing catch,*Lk 5:4*

Calming wind-whipped waves with simple rebuke,*Mark 4:35*

    Each mir'cle terrifying who knew him,*Mark 4:41*

Like sailors throwing Noah overboard

To instantly calm Lord's raging storm.*Jonah 1:15*

Look around you at the Father's power,*Rom 1:20*

The same power brought the Son back to life,*1Co 6:14*

Then rely on his power, not your own,*1Co 2:5*

That of his doing immeasur'bly more

Than all we of God ask or imagine,*Eph 3:20*

Supply forever to carry good news,*Eph 3:7*

Although incomparably greater One,*Eph 1:18*

Not might nor power but his Spirit,*Zech 4:5*

Water walk,*Matt 14:32* not magic but miracle,*John 6:21*

Evident Creator walked among us,*John 2:23*

Stunning you with wonder after wonder,*John 7:21*

So that all with eyes knew his origin.

Thus learn from your ancestors who spurned

The one great God who then scattered bodies

Afar lost in desperate wilderness,*1Co 10:5*

Having tested Son and died forever for it.*1Co 10:9*

Grumble not against great rescuer King,

Lest you, like unsaved ancestors, lose all.*1Co 10:10*

Light

Light, glorious light, saturating light,

Father created and embedded light,*Jn 1:4*

Imbued with care, but man corrupted with

One-thousand hates, a million evils,

Light against dark, life against death, battling;

Yet life won over death when Son rose 'gain,

Father holding life's power over all,*Jn 11:25*

As herald John told you the Son is light,*Jn 1:6*

Shedding the Father's light on actions all,*Jn 3:21*

    Son's light feeding you to eternal life,*Jn 6:32*

His body, food and drink, sustaining you,*Jn 6:34*

    As your earthly repast could never do,

For with other you die, while with him live,*Jn 6:48*

    Son living in Father, you 'live in Son,*Jn 14:19*

Light shining even where God plunged Pharaoh

    Into immob'lizing blackest darkness,*Exo 10:23*

Olive-oil Holy Spirit lamps burning*Exo 27:20*

    Continually, at Father's rich command,*Lev 24:2*

The Lord your lamp, deepest darkness turned day,*2Sam 22:29*

    God giving light to eyes blind from bondage,*Ezra 9:8*

Lord your salvation light, of whom to fear,*Psalm 27:1*

    Life's fountain, in whose light you see more light,*Psalm 36:9*

People stumbling in night's pitch seeing

    Great light dawning over harrowing land.*Isaiah 9:2*

Spiritual, and constant glad for it,*Jn 6:63*

    You also have the Son's different peace,*Jn 14:27*

Abundant peace from the Father and Son,*1Pe 1:2*

    Quiet and confident,*2Co 1:2* easygoing,*Ro 1:7*

Salving mind's ease where raw wounds painful burned,*2Ti 1:2*

    Inwardly still although outward riven,*Lk 12:51*

One new peaceful humanity he made,*Eph 2:15*

    Between insider and outsider,*Eph 2:17*

One Spirit, all with access one Father,*Eph 2:18*

    For those choosing to follow the Son's light.*Jn 12:36*

The Father lives always in brilliant light,

Unapproachably powerful, lustrous,_{1Ti 6:15}

Intimating no least hint of darkness,_{1Jn 1:5}

Could e'er inhabit immortality._{2Ti 1:10}

As Father transfigured Son on high mount,

Before utter speechless Peter, James, John,_{Mark 9:2}

Only the Son's light makes things visible;

Everything Son illuminates is light._{Eph 5:13}

So we joyfully live in Father's light,

Fulfilling all hope while battling darkness,

Living in harmony as one body,_{Eph 4:4}

Grown strong in Lord's peace, full Spirit helping,_{Acts 9:31}

Sovereign Lord our strength, our sore feet made

Like those of deer to tread on highest heights,_{Hab 3:19}

Thinking alike, all having same love mind,_{1Pe 3:8}

Accepting one another as Son you._{Ro 15:7}

Poor in body while rich Father and Son,_{Rev 2:9}

Body Son-kept true in corrupt culture,_{Rev 2:13}

Not lukewarm to Son, better hot or cold,_{Rev 3:15}

Wretched, pitiful, poor, blind, and naked._{Rev 3:16}

Darkness

Everyone who follows the Son sees,_{Jn 12:46}

His light prevailing in the world's darkness._{Jn 1:5}

Though Son shines his light on the world's darkness,

People turn from the light, wanting darkness,_{Jn 3:19}

Hating the Son's great light while loving wrongs,_{Jn 3:20}

Wrongs that can only happen in darkness,_{Jn 9:4}

People living in death's darkest shadow

11

When rejecting the dawn of Son's great light,*Matt 4:13*

Isaiah foretold half millenium

Before history's epochal Christ dawn.*Isa 9:2*

For darkness had man ardently pursued,

In wicked sin, Sodom and Gomorrah,*Gen 13:13*

Though first formed in Lord's well-watered garden,*Gen 13:10*

E'en Israel sacrificing sons, daughters,*2Kings 17:17*

To worship cast idol calves and Ash'rah poles,

Bow to starry hosts, divine dark omens,*2Kings 17:16*

Prostituting their souls on high places,*Ezek 16:16*

Rejecting the holy One for their false gods

Baal,*Jdg 2:11* Molek,*1Kings 11:7* Ashtoreth, even Chemosh,*1Kings 11:33*

Jezebels all, killing the Lord's prophets,*1Kings 18:4*

Senseless, shamed by their own crafted idols,

Their formed images merely breathless frauds,*Jer 10:14*

Yet dogs to devour, utter avenged shame,*2Kings 9:36*

Loving not God's light but utter darkness,

Even to betray God's begotten Son,

Enemy not fought but courted, welcomed

Into Judas' soul for thirty pence won,*Matt 26:15*

Cast into temple for potter's field done,*Matt 27:3*

On tree to hang like of rejected Son,*Matt 27:5*

Evil soul darkness pursued, lost though won,

To serpent's query, does God really say

Anything of eternal consequence?*Gen 3:1*

Beguiling Eve whose offer man welcomed,*Gen 3:6*

Eyes opened, naked seen, to hide from God,*Gen 3:5*

As wife mocked good Job for holding fast his

Integrity, rather curse God and die,*Job 2:9*

For better to live on your roof's corner

    Than share your house with a quarrelsome wife.*Prov 25:24*

God created mankind upright and pure,

    But off man went searching profitless schemes,*Ecc 7:29*

Sin nature fixed at first birth, corrupt, twisted,

    Every inclination only evil,*Gen 6:5*

Until God would wash earth's face in regret,*Gen 6:7*

    'Cept Noah find favor in the Lord's eyes,*Gen 6:8*

Two by two into ark*Gen 6:19* to float on flood

    Of forty day-night rains,*Gen 7:17* creation save,

After raven haunt*Gen 8:7* until dove alight,*Gen 8:12*

    Drawn gently out of ark 'gain multiply,*Gen 8:17*

Rainbow sheltered sure God's covenant sign,

    Never recur to destroy all earth's life,*Gen 9:13*

As Abr'am carried circumcision as

    Father's everlasting covenant sign.*Gen 17:11*

Watch you, watch for those who pretend ally,

    When seeking to destroy your devotion,*Matt 7:15*

'Zekiel's watchman be for your people,*Ezekiel 33:2*

    Standing upon rampart trumpet to blow,*Ezekiel 33:6*

When seeing sword coming to repay wrong,

    Give warning, give warning! Your people save!*Ezekiel 33:7*

Lest leave scattered, dry bones on valley floor,*Ezekiel 37:2*

    No Spirit to breathe life into stooped troops,*Ezekiel 37:10*

No rattling sound, dry bones come together,

    No vast Israelite forces to their feet.*Ezek 37:11*

Choose not your own destructive delusion,*2Th 2:11*

Chattering idly to become more idle,*2Ti 2:17*

The one who confuses paying all due,*Gal 5:9*

Enemies pretending one's friends to be.*2Co 11:15*

Walk with Son and darkness never walk be,*Jn 8:12*

No daylight stumble, only in darkness,*Jn 11:9*

The Son's light for you for little longer,*Jn 12:34*

When to walk in dark is nowhere to be.*Jn 12:35*

Persevere through darkness, mature, complete,*Jas 1:2*

To learn compassion, suffering bare brief,*1Pe 1:6*

For the Lord's compassions never fail but

Renew 'gain ev'ry dawn out of great love,*Lam 3:22*

Son's own, coaxing your enduring hardship,*2Th 3:5*

As Job did not sin, when he refused to

Charge God for Satan's awful destruction,*Job 1:22*

Then character won, and with it hope,*Ro 5:3*

God's own angels having guarded your way,*Psa 91:11*

No one but the Father, his all to win,*Heb 13:6*

Placing enmity between Satan and

His beguiled man, Son to crush Satan's head,*Gen 3:15*

As Satan roams throughout earth, dark phantom

Breathing death on it, pursuit man's torment.*Job 2:2*

Light and darkness nothing in common have;*2Co 6:14*

Darkness hides no evil from light's sure sight,*Mk 4:21*

The Father seeing all, plain-day to him,*Heb 4:13*

Whispered in dark good as shouted rooftop.*Lk 12:2*

All evil only thus admit and cease,

Defeated in Son's all-powerful light.

People

But what to make of creation other

    Than true that God also created man,*Gen 1:27*

And did so in his own holy image,*Jas 1:18*

    Male and female he made them in image,*Gen 1:27*

Alone not good, so out of sleeper's rib

    Glory woman made, bone of bone, flesh flesh,*Gen 2:23*

Lonely hearts joined in mar'tal sacrament,*Gen 2:21*

    Leaving, cleaving, becoming one godly flesh,*Gen 2:24*

Father blessed to be fruitful, multiply,*Gen 1:28* as

    As highest form, not soulless animal,

In Father's own likeness, like that of Son,*Acts 17:29*

    Never to curse another who likewise

Likeness bears, same glor'ous Father and Son,*Jas 3:9*

    Nor to curse the potter who molded made,*Ro 9:19*

The formed rejecting the One forming it,*Isaiah 29:16*

    Pot saying potter neither knows nor 'xist,

Free will exercise, loving or spurning

    Gracious God who granted it knowing so,

Making lifeless images to worship,

    Unconscious cons to shame, not save, maker,*Jer 51:17*

No freewill offering made him to praise,*Psalm 54:6*

    But through own creation inward pursue

Own self to bitter narciss'stic dead end,

    Having lost the truth that forever frees.*John 8:36*

God made you to honor Father and Son,*1Pe 4:13*

    Rescued you to worship him who made you*Eph 1:5*

Like him, joined with him, supplying your need,*Col 3:10*

Knowing him through what he alone has made,_{Ro 1:20}

Transformed bit by bit closer his image,

Daily greater glory from his Spirit,_{2Cor 3:18}

Not condemned but loved as very children,_{Lk 16:8}

His kindness cords leading you, love binding,

Child lifted to God's cheek, bent down feed you,_{Hosea 11:4}

Unless you reject his own chosen Son._{Ro 10:16}

Some feel no need of him,_{Matt 8:33} others sell out,_{Matt 26:14}

Disowning him who must then disown them,_{Lk 12:9}

Turnabout fair play,_{2Ti 2:12} either with or 'gainst,_{Lk 11:23}

No other good-news rescue come for you;_{Gal 1:6}

Good news must soon crush those who reject it._{1Pe 2:7}

So tell, shout good news! Son to brag of you,_{Matt 10:32}

Train your lamp on the Father, light to shine,_{Lk 11:34}

As Father lights you, your deeds exposed, true,_{Lk 11:35}

Chosen, though, out of your nowhere, nothing,_{1Pe 2:9}

His vital light pouring into, through you._{2Co 4:6}

No easy thing, this turn, hardly for Son,_{Matt 8:19}

Trials and suff'ring instead before you,_{Mk 13:9}

Scorned by all, despised, worm not man, so Son,_{Psa 22:6}

Mocked, insulted, pierced for your transgression,_{Psa 22:7}

Poured like water, bones disjoint, on display,_{Psa 22:14}

Naked, garment soldiers cast lot divide,_{Psa 22:18}

What good news should be, fam'lies asunder,_{Matt 10:21}

Him despised, so rejecting your old ways,_{Lk 14:25}

Opposition as opportunity,_{Lk 21:12}

Good news to share, easily worth its cost,_{Lk 14:26}

Way forward neither hard nor myster'ous,_{Php 4:3}

Doing right things to please your glad Father,*Eph 5:8*

Holding to word with your life depending,*Php 2:15*

In a world of such distinct light and dark.*1Jn 2:9-11*

Dawn comes whether you wake to it or not,*Ro 13:12*

So let light liven you,*1Th 3:8* not darkness drown,*1Th 5:5*

Living happily in King's paradise,*Col 1:12*

Thanking the Father for others dwell, too,

You, the world's light! Honor Father, not you.*Matt 5:14*

Actions determine your fate with Father,*Matt 21:28*

Doing mattering more than your talking,*Matt 21:30*

Turning from sin far more than past sinning.*Matt 21:32*

Your Father rewards those who do his work,*Mk 12:9*

So stand firm, moved not least from his planned good,*Eph 2:10*

To always give yourself sacrific'lly

To your Father's work, no effort wasted.

Book 2: Creator

Transcendent

To share Father, Son, and Spirit story,

> Essential for your one eternal life,

Embrace Father's transcendent attributes,

> Before, beyond, above, ending all things,*Rev 1:8*

While instant nourishing you as his child,*Rev 21:6*

> Treating past past for those Son relying,*1Ti 1:2*

Utterly compassionate, grace unearned,*1Th 5:28*

> Free of guilt, though guilty, Spirit no blame.*Heb 10:29*

God's character is your sole liberty,*2Ti 1:9*

> Freed not for who you are but 'stead he is,*Ro 2:24*

Allowing your wrongs to prove his kindness,*Ro 11:32*

> His compassion strengthening your resolve.*Heb 13:9*

Yahweh went before fleeing Israelites,

> Feared pillar of day cloud and fire night,*Exo 13:21*

Strangest smoking firepot and blazing torch,

> In dreadful darkness 'twixt blood sacrifice,*Gen 15:17*

Ascending in flame of Manoah's fire,*Jdg 13:20*

> Glory settled forty days Mount Sinai top,*Exo 24:16*

Fearsome 'cause unbased, numinous, apart,

> But yet in your jealous rescue pursuit,*Ro 10:20*

Great shepherd earn'st not to lose even one,*1Ti 2:3*

 Satan trapped in deadly pitch-black ravine,

Son to draw you into his gorgeous light,*1Pe 2:9*

 Made extraord'nary out of dust nothing.*Col 1:12*

God sends but transcends wind, earthquake, and fire,*1Kings 19:11*

 To gently whisper in ear, calm your fear,*1Kings 19:12*

And then quakes again at Son's brief demise,*Matt 27:54*

 To roll back tomb's awful stone, angel top,*Matt 28:2*

Sunder chain locks, throw open prison doors,*Acts 16:26*

 Always above, beyond, wonders, awe, more,

Willing, desiring, chasing, hunting his,*Ro 10:21*

 Wanting that you know certain he exist,

Earnestly seek him in faith, as he you,

 Expecting from him full unearned reward,*Heb 11:6*

As patriarch Abram sought unknown parts,*Heb 11:8*

 Obeying in Harran the Lord's hard word,*Gen 12:1*

Confident to live in promised strange land,*Heb 11:9*

 With wife Sarai confident child to bear,*Heb 11:11*

Just as Father rewards your trust in him,*Gal 3:8*

 The Father's power fulfilling promise.*Ro 4:18*

Sovereign

Reign superior to all author'ty,*Gal 3:8*

 Unlimited, free to command as fit,*1Th 2:12*

Ruler of all things, all wealth and honor,

 All strength and power, in his mighty hands,*1Chr 29:12*

Sovereign Lord elevating Daniel

 In king's favor over all Babylon,*Dan 2:48*

Elevating Joseph over Egypt,*Acts 7:10*

    Grant Solomon more wisdom than e'er known,*1Kings 4:34*

That Sheba's Queen would honor him with great

    Caravan gold for answ'ring her questions,*1Kings 10:1*

Mordecai on king's horse for honor robed,*Esth 7:11*

    Each accounting God's sovereign power,

Each righteous, mortal only for own sin,

    Rather than sins of a parent or child,*Ezek 18:4*

Yet all returning to the most high God,

    All kingdoms under his highest heaven.*Dan 7:27*

Remarkable that he counts you as worthy,*2Th 1:5*

    Death's escape from Sovereign Lord alone,*Psa 68:20*

When Father had no need to share his rule,*Col 1:12*

    His inestimable invitation*2Ti 4:1*

To share all his, as you give all yourself,*2Ti 4:18*

    Not food alone but his everything,*Ro 14:17*

Complete submission, entirely his,*Heb 10:22*

    Confident among others in good news,*1Th 3:10*

Household providing as believers do,*1Ti 5:8*

    Your faith reinforcing and reinforced.*Heb 6:12*

Ahaz refused command a sign to ask,*Isa 7:11*

    So Isaiah the virgin birth foretold,

God come among his people, Immanuel,*Isa 7:14*

    Not summoning stormy mount, blazing fire,*Heb 12:18*

But wondrous city filled with joyful life,*Heb 12:22*

    Throngs celebrating Father and Son love,*Heb 12:23*

Planned before creation, perfect par'dise,*Eph 1:4*

    Perfectly forgiven, never embarrassing,*Heb 11:16*

Working for his ever greater reward,*Lk 19:24*

    Yet as his children, dependent on him,*Lk 9:48*

No favorites,*Heb 1:8* just his arms open wide,*1Pe 1:10*

    Sharing his rule generously with you,*Col 1:12*

God, not man who on whim changes his mind,*Psa 110:4*

    The Glory of Israel, not man who lies,*1Sam 15:29*

Ezekiel's vision, lapis-lazuli

    Throne,*Ezek 1:26* waist up like molten metal, fire below,*Ezek 1:27*

Surround of brilliant light, radiant rainbow,

    Fearful prophet falling facedown,*Ezek 1:28* or of

Daniel's vision, linen-dressed, fine-gold belt,*Dan 10:5*

    Topaz torso, lightning-lit face, torch eyes,

Burnished-bronze arms and legs, multitude voice,*Dan 10:6*

    All his absolute sovereignty declare.

Word

Our alien God stranger still is as Word,

    Beginning as Word with God, as God,*Jn 1:1*

Flesh taken to walk human among us,*Jn 1:14*

    Word full of Spirit, words sustaining life,

When flesh counts nothing, only Spirit life,*Jn 6:63*

    Communicating his shocking marvel,*Eph 3:3*

Saying light, comes light,*Gen 1:3* land apart from water,*Gen 1:6*

    Saying seed, comes plant,*Gen 1:11* saying day and night,*Gen 1:14*

Saying creatures and fowl,*Gen 1:24* saying mankind rule,*Gen 1:26*

    Fruitful to be over ev'ry creature.*Gen 1:28*

Word also law, eye for eye, tooth for tooth,*Exo 21:24*

    Protecting property*Exo 22:1* pure relations,*Exo 22:16*

Ensuring justice with ample mercy,*Exo 23:1*

  Compassionate justice, saving, building,*Zech 7:10*

Not oppressing fatherless or widow,*Zech 7:10*

  Glor'ously summed in nation-making form,

Commandments ten from Mount Sinai reaches,*Exo 20:1*

  No other gods, no idols, not profane,

On Sabbath to rest, honor give parents,

  Not murder, nor adultery, nor steal,*Exo 20:3*

Moses carried on tablets down,*Exo 24:12* to break

  Over cast golden calf, enslavers' god!*Exo 32:19*

Yet so word devoted, acacia ark

  Tablets to make,*Exo 25:16* Uzzah's irrevent touch

God's wrath his life to take,*2Sam 6:7* so venerate

  God's holy word, no stumbling oxen make,

David 'stead danced ark to Jerusalem,

  As wife Michal window peered, despised him,*1Chron 15:29*

Nor captured covenant ark, false Dagon

  God keep, like tumor-afflicted Ashdod.*1Samuel 5:7*

Father of meaning, Father of Son Word,

  Whispers, commands, wanting you know his will

To form you as spiritual being,*Jas 1:17*

  Reflecting his glory, as conscious soul,

To pursue his precious intimacy,*2Ti 2:22*

  Listening, hearing, obeying in love,*Ro 6:16*

Filled of his goodness,*Ro 15:14* diff'rent, apart, right,*Matt 5:13*

  Wielding word as his pure parsing-heart sword,*Eph 6:17*

Accepting his Spirit striving in you,*1Th 2:13*

  Welcoming his words as great gifts they are,*1Ti 4:5*

Irresistible heart-scorching ardor,

    Embedded in bones, your tongue cannot hold,*Jer 20:9*

Though speaker bound tight, God's word winging free,*2Ti 2:9*

    Informing, reforming, transforming you,*2Ti 3:16*

Not aimless talk but imparting wisdom,*1Co 1:5*

    Wondrous words of faith fellowship for you.

God's words wrought time, space, energy, matter,*Jn 1:3*

    Then made living-Word Son, truth embodied,*Jn 1:14*

So Son should show just what Father told him,*Jn 3:32*

    God's word gone forth, prevailed,*Ro 9:6* alive in you,*Heb 4:12*

Rich words for your ready tongue, not just know,*2Co 4:13*

    Sharing words before quotidian do,*Acts 6:1*

That flourishing may follow, gospel spread,*Acts 12:24*

    Flown forth from Father's mouth, purpose clear borne,

Accomplishing all that he most desires,

    Never word returning to him empty,*Isa 55:11*

But once spoken, then done, to trust, rely,*Rev 21:5*

    God having spoken future back in time,

As Mordecai counseled Esther speak at

    Moment, lest deliverance come elsewhere.*Esther 4:14*

Fall prostrate on hearing breathtaking word,

    On miracle vision from Almighty,*Numbers 24:4*

Crediting, acknowledging, revering.*Deut 17:19*

    Draw near to hear whispered revelation,*Josh 3:9*

Lest his words work witness hard against you;*Josh 24:27*

    Flawless are his words in which to shelter,*2Sam 22:31*

Coming to prophets Nathan,*1Chron 17:3* Shemaiah,*2Chron 11:2*

    Ne'er to wither but endure forever.*Isa 40:8*

Father

Glory that Creator reveals his thoughts,*Amos 4:13*

    Not as phantom force but loving Father,

Not among many fathers but your One,*Matt 23:2*

    God o'er ev'rything, simultan'ous near,

Abba Father, personal, intimate,*Mk 14:36*

    Show'ring gifts on beloved sons and daughters,*2Co 6:18*

Eager awaits, you join him etern'lly,*Eph 3:14*

    Wise children who worship only Father,

Not Satan enemy, father of lies,*Jn 8:44*

    But genuine friend, our holy Father,

Shown in Abr'am, God's chosen faith father,*Ro 4:11*

    Sire of all those who pursue God's promise,*Ro 4:16*

Nations' father,*Gen 17:4* though Abr'am fall laughing, *Eph 17:17*

    As wife Sarai laughed,*Gen 18:12* mother of nations,*Gen 17:16*

Yet God's covenant certainly be yours,

    Though distant children of Abr'am's promise,*Ro 9:8*

Abraham, descended from Noah through

    Semite father Shem,*Gen 11:26* called to promised land,*Gen 12:1*

With Sarah, father of Isaac, father of

    Jacob, father of twelve roy'l patriarchs,*1Chron 2:1*

From them Messiah's human ancestry

    Traced, God over all, forever to praise.*Ro 9:5*

God centered earth, tiny vast-racing orb,*Eph 3:10*

    Elevating his image human'ty,

His reign universal, one author'ty,

    His body all who rely on his Son,*1Co 1:2*

His members caring for one another,*1Ti 5:16*

    Wrinkle free, blameless, from Son sacrifice.*Eph 5:25*

How beautiful you are and how pleasing,

    My beloved, with your delights,*Song 7:6* to him belong;

Who is this coming up from wilderness,

    Leaning so heavily on her beloved?*Song 8:5*

Father's body a profound mystery,*Eph 5:32*

    Each of you different 'ssential part,*Ro 12:5*

Formed and vitalized to work together,*Eph 4:12*

    Each equally important role, function,*1Co 12:15*

None rejecting another, weak or strong,*1Co 12:21*

    Each indispens'ble, honorable all,*1Co 12:22*

Suffering for one another, Father,*1Th 2:14*

    As any body's members must suffer.

You meet the Father solely through his Son,*Matt 11:27*

    God comprehensed only as a Father,

Fam'ly as the universe's one source,*Heb 1:5*

    Father naming Son, claiming fatherhood*Heb 5:5*

To shelter, guard, comfort, guide his children,*1Th 2:5*

    Help his children,*2Th 3:3* nourishing,*1Ti 4:6* rewarding,*Heb 11:6*

As perfect Father would cherished children,

    Nothing impossible for the faithful,*Matt 17:20*

Within God's utter sacrificial love,

    Having given his own Son to win you,*Ro 8:32*

Son advocating with Father for you,*1Jn 2:1*

    As in fam'ly most-loving sibling would,*1Jn 4:15*

None judging and rejecting another,

    As no family could,*1Jn 4:17* crying instead,

One to another, in passionate heart,*Ro 8:15*

> Daddy dearest, Father, ready to give,*Gal 4:6*

To swift secure cup from Son, all poss'ble,

> Yet not our desire but his good be done.*Mk 14:36*

Family also rules, Son over all,*Heb 2:5*

> Father-installed, reciprocal honor,*2Pe 1:17*

Son holding authority over all,*Matt 28:18*

> Speaking in his Father's sovereign stead,*Jn 14:10*

Teaching, reaching,*Mk 1:21* healing*Lk 5:17* with author'ty,

> To grant 'ternal life to those Father gave,*Jn 17:2*

Special invitation, not hard harsh rule,*Matt 22:1*

> Accepted only who know their deep need,*Matt 22:7*

Many invited, few choosing his rule,*Matt 22:11*

> Excuse made, none good,*Lk 14:16* to prefer other,*1Th 2:12*

Son then to destroy all contrary rule,

> Returning power to holy Father.*1Co 15:24*

Spirit

Our transcendent God is also Spirit,

> Reaching you, ev'dent in his Son's essence,*Ro 5:5*

Able so to live in you, you in him,

> As only Spirit can: close, companion,

Conscience, comfort, counsel, true, trusted, touched,*Ro 8:14*

> To gently pursue spiritual things,

Your voice plaintive child rather than demand,*Ro 8:15*

> Sibling to Son rather than stark enemy,*Ro 8:16*

Spirit advocating, defending you,*Ro 8:27*

> Father then to lavish honor on you.*Ro 8:17*

Spirit goes beyond mind, will, emotion,

>Touching conscience to reject enemy,*1Jn 4:4*

Warning against self-seeking deception,

>Condemning the enemy's worldly view*1Ti 4:1*

That you are chance dust, fast to dust return,*1Jn 4:5*

>For the Son's truth that you are his spirit,*1Co 12:8*

God destined for his spiritual realm,

>Welcoming paradise news of the Son.*Heb 1:7*

So submit only to Father's Spirit,*Heb 12:9*

>Made perfect, in Spirit truly to live,*Heb 12:23*

Keeping Spirit's oil constantly burning

>That the Lord may dwell richly among you.*Exo 27:21*

Oh, Father! Cast us not from your presence,

>Neither deny us your Holy Spirit;*Psa 51:11*

Let us not rebel, grieving your Spirit,*Isa 63:10*

>That we would turn en'my 'gainst you to fight,

But let Spirit dwell like Belteshazzar,*Dan 4:18*

>Daniel's holy 'telligence and wisdom,*Dan 5:11*

Conceiving Son in us as conceived Mary,*Matt 1:18*

>Baptized of the Father, Son, and Spirit,*Matt 28:19*

As Spirit filled Zechariah,*Lk 1:67* 'Lizbeth,*Lk 1:41*

>Simeon,*Lk 2:25* all to witness Son's coming,

Samson to strike dead with donkey jawbone

>One-thousand shouting Philistines soldiers,*Jdg 15:14*

Saul to rescue Jabesh Gilead men

>Surrendered to sure Ammonite slaughter,*1Sam 11:6*

Spirit then temporar'ly filling them,

>Until God would pour out self-same Spirit,*Isa 44:3*

No long to depart but in mouths to dwell,*Isa 59:21*

    Permanently, in gift tongues of fire.*Acts 2:3*

Sanctify us, oh Spirit, saving us,*2Thess 2:13*

    Through your daily washing with God's own word.

Reconciler

God, reconciling, loves peace, unity

    First removing divide 'tween you and him,*Php 1:2*

Neither tyrant nor fearsome war monger,

    Eschewing harsh judgment sin deserves, for

Reli'ble love,*2Jn 3:1* unmerited favor,*Gal 3:1*

    Offer his confidence, warmth, secur'ty,*Jude 1*

Old scores forgiven, reconcil'ation*2Co 5:18*

    For all things everywhere, Son to himself,*Col 1:20*

Made good again, in heaven and on earth,

    To embrace corrupted world, Son made clean,

Pleased you share his offer expensive love,*2Co 5:19*

    Not end the world's self-induced misery,

No second Noah's flood, start o'er again,*Gen 10:32*

    Rainbow promise, his covenant he kept,*Gen 9:16*

Tranquil'ty, peace, contentment, happiness,*Col 1:2*

    In the Father you find these desir'd things.*1Th 1:1*

Listen, heed his dearest-bought offer peace,*2Th 1:1*

    Father your only way, reconciler,*2Ti 1:2*

Israel's vict'ries not righteousness but the

    Lord's righteousness and others' wickedness,*Deut 9:4*

As prophet Hosea took wife Gomer

    Out of prostitution at Lord's command,*Hosea 1:2*

His forgiving kindness restoring her,

As God restores his adult'rous people,*Hosea 1:10*

He who finds a wife finding what is good,

While also receiving the Lord's favor,*Prov 18:22*

And as David counted his fighting men

Against Lord's will, resulting nation plagued,*2Sam 24:10*

'Til David bought Araunah's threshing floor,*2Sam 24:21*

For altar sacrifice, reconciled God.*2Sam 24:25*

Hold nothing against brother or sister,

The Father holding nothing against you;*Lk 6:36*

Let things go, honoring Father for you,*Matt 9:13*

As Son submitted to Father's judgment

So that Father could let you clean-free go,*Ro 15:8*

As you must let go others lest 'gainst you.*Jas 2:12*

Father reconciles the worst to show Son

Special indeed, so cap'ble of rescue,*1Ti 1:16*

As to make you want to do your own good,*Ro 12:1*

Sanctification called, simpler answered,

Cleaned of all sin, pulled from death's cold hard grip,*Jn 6:39*

Drawn to paradise, forever with Son,*Jn 6:40*

Drawn of whispers in desperate last days,*Jn 6:44*

Yours alone, none other, to heed his call,*Jn 6:65*

Useless without, like Jeremiah's belt,*Jer 13:7*

Bound to God but not listening to him.*Jer 13:11*

As Father drew Son back to his throne side,

In charge again over all, forever,*Eph 1:19*

So he draws you back to him forever,*1Jn 5:11*

Great gift of life, of eternal living,*1Jn 5:13*

Permanent, good forever, not fancied,*2Th 2:16*

    Unprecedented compassion shown you,*2Co 1:3*

Your best opportunity for him now,*Co 6:2*

    Father giving his only Son for you

To live forever,*Jn 3:16* ancient writing filled,*Mk 1:1*

    Only immortality for mortals,*Jn 14:4*

Rescued, reconciled, restored, and renewed,

    All for relying on the Son's good news.*mk 1:14*

Restorer

When the Lord met Sol'mon at Gibeon,

    Saying to ask for whatever wanted,*1Kings 3:5*

And Solomon asked only for wisdom,*1Kings 3:9*

    He pleased the Lord to give him riches, too,*1Kings 3:13*

Just as you should ask for the Lord's approach,

    Even if you desire to receive else,

Knowing that if you cast glance at riches,

    They sprout wings, flying off like an eagle,*Prov 23:5*

Because the Lord doesn't just rescue you

    But restores you, revives you, makes you new,*Ro 6:3*

Animates you with his Son's transcendence,

    Seen walking right out of your sure grave, too,

Same Spirit raising you from dead to 'live,*Ro 8:11*

    Perfect, holy, acceptable to him.*Ro 4:25*

As the Father restored Job to full health

    And in far greater fortune than before,*Job 42:10*

The Father restores you incorrupt'ble,*1Pe 1:3*

Not temp'rary, partial, but ever, full,*Col 2:13*

Wanting you all awake, alive, not dead,*Col 3:1*

New life remaining hidden in the Son,*Col 3:3*

But wait, you'll see it when the Son returns,*1Th 1:10*

Forgiving Father, perm'nent perfect fix,

Know who he is, transforming character!

Your one restorer making new again,

As God moved Pharaoh to restore Joseph,*Gen 41:41*

After brothers sold their dreamer as slave,*Gen 37:5*

As God restored Moses' white-diseased hand*Ex 4:7*

After rebuke over his disbelief,*Exo 4:4*

Jeroboam's outstretched shriveled-up hand,*1Kings 13:6*

In Jordan waters, Namaan's leprosy,*2Kings 5:14*

For returning to God always restores,*Job 22:23*

Flesh renewed as in long ago youth days.*Job 33:25*

Son prayed that Father not separate them,

And Father answered, giving Son new life,*Heb 5:7*

Beating for you your worst enemy death,*1Co 15:26*

As ancient witness said, three days back again,*1Co 15:3*

The Son human because you are human,

His only way your own death to defeat,*Heb 2:14*

Your curse on his back, his death to pay back,*Gal 3:13*

Your sad wrongs, your sadness leading to Son.*2Co 7:10*

Giver

Who else is this extr'ordinary God?

He is giver, beyond comprehension,*Eph 1:13*

Marking you not spray symbol, gang tattoo,

But himself, Holy Spirit inside you,

Ensuring you receive his ev'rything,

Gifted him, his greatest possible gift.*Tit 5:6*

Give like your Father, when poor counting more,*Mk 12:41*

Sell your many things to give,*Lk 12:33* pleasing God

To give back that which was already his,*Ro 11:35*

For God is your giver, attending poor

As gen'rously as rich,*Jas 2:2* good news wanting

More than enslaving wealthy exploiters,*Jas 2:5*

Joyful poverty rich gen'rosity,*2Co 8:2*

Having nothing, possessing ev'rything,*2Co 6:8*

Pleasing Father while rejoicing in Son,*Matt 19:16*

Sharing one another's grief and struggles,*Php 4:14*

Giving beyond abil'ty,*2Co 8:3* Father first,

Then to others, above expectation,*2Co 8:4*

Excelling,*2Co 8:7* sharing what was always his,*2Co 9:11*

Willing, cheerful, not under compulsion,*2Co 9:7*

Your gift opening doors to his presence,*Prov 18:16*

Returning his gifts of seed-bearing fruit,*Gen 1:29*

Ev'rlasting possession of fertile lands,*Gen 17:8*

Lands overflowing with milk and honey,*Lev 20:24*

Heaven's dew among earth's rich abundance,*Gen 27:28*

As Joseph gave brothers God's sacked treasure,*Gen 43:23*

Indeed, giving breath to all living things,*Num 27:16*

That we give in return only one tenth.*Gen 28:22*

The Father gives wisely for most ben'fit,*1Th 4:8*

His Spirit giving you power, control,*2Ti 1:7*

    Genuine, effective, in Son's witness,*Ro 15:18*

        Spirit showing you other of his gifts,*1Co 2:9*

Searching ev'rything of Father's for you,*1Co 2:10*

        Knowing Father's thoughts to share them with you,*1Co 2:11*

His thought ways so much higher than your ways,

        His word always accomplishing his purpose,*Isa 55:11*

You knowing the Father's wonders for you,*1Co 2:12*

        Freed even from death's fear, what bigger gift

Could be?*Heb 2:15* then to come back to life again,*Ro 8:11*

    Not enslaved but in literal heaven.

Lover

Love stands first 'mong God's limitless qualities,

    'Bove all, God as love, first, last, and alone,*1Jn 4:16*

The Father knowing well those who love him,*1Co 8:3*

    Far as you love because Father loved you,*1Jn 4:19*

Love coming from the Father, defining,*1Jn 4:7*

    Those not loving not knowing the Father

Because the Father is agape love,*1Jn 4:8*

    Shown freely to a thousand gen'rations,*Ex 20:6*

For those who love him, keeping his commands,

    So when you love others, Father is in you.*1Jn 4:12*

The Father teaches to love each other,*1Th 4:9-10*

    To treat foreigner as if native-born,*Lev 19:34*

Be slow to anger, abounding in love,*Num 14:18*

    God's Spirit pouring his love over you,*Ro 5:5*

In electric embrace others must feel,*Gal 5:22*

    Father loving whoever loves the Son.*Jn 14:21*

Love one another as the Son loves you,*Jn 13:34*

    Not as Samson lusted for Delilah,*Jdg 16:4*

And fell captive to her treach'rous wiles,*Jdg 16:19*

    Nor as Solomon took seven-hundred

Wives who turned his heart after other gods,*1Kings 11:4*

    The heart deceitful above all things and

Beyond man's cure, although God examined,*Jer 17:9*

    But the Lord's eternal love for Israel,*1Kings 10:9*

Not fickle but enduring forever,*1Chron 16:34*

    Love that invites you into God's own house,*Psa 5:7*

Love that follows you all of your life's day,*Psa 23:6*

    A love showing others you know the Son,*Jn 13:35*

Doing for others as you wish for you,*Matt 7:12*

    Loving Father with mind, will, emotion,*Matt 22:34*

While loving neighbor as you love yourself,*Mk 12:31*

    Doing as Son says, showing who loves him.*Jn 14:21*

Love as the Son loved you,*Jn 15:12* ev'rything love,*1Co 16:14*

    Spurring one another toward love, his love,*Heb 10:24*

As brothers and sisters, fam'ly motive,*Heb 13:1*

    Taken thus from death to life in great trust,*1Jn 3:11-14*

Confident in Son, conscience clear for love,*1Ti 1:5*

    Example for others,*1Ti 4:11* love increasing,*2Th 1:3*

Giving yourself for others,*Jn 15:13* devoted,*Ro 12:10*

    So, reducing another's corruption,*1Pe 4:8*

Like a mother loving child,*1Th 2:7-8* sincerely,*Ro 12:9*

Deeply, from the heart,*1Pe 1:22* building others up.*1Co 8:1*

Nothing separates you from the Son's love,*Ro 8:35*

Nor from the Father's love, given Son for you,*Ro 8:38*

As God asked Abra'm to give his son Isaac,*Gen 22:2*

Save for the thicket ram's blood, sacrificed,*Gen 22:13*

To foreshadow the Father's sacrifice

Of his only begotten, his one Son,

Son given so that you could live through him,*1Jn 4:9*

Rescued from yourself*1Jn 4:10* only by Son's love,*Jn 13:1*

Son loving you as Father loved his Son,*Jn 15:9*

So that you can love even enemies,*Lk 6:27-28*

Letting enemies wrong without return,*Matt 5:38*

Going extra miles for worst enemy,*Matt 5:41*

Not a noisy love,*1Co 13:1* not a brilliant love,*1Co 13:2*

But patient, kind, without envy or boast,*1Co 13:4*

Not seeking self or easily angered,*1Co 13:5*

But rejoicing in truth,*1Co 13:6* trusting, hoping,*1Co 13:7*

Never failing, even when all else stops,*1Co 13:8*

And nothing remains but you, Father, Son,

To love the Lord your God with all your heart,

With all your soul, strength, and understanding.*Deut 6:5*

Supreme

Paul told Athen'an Areopagus,*Acts 17:19*

Truth that no man's hands can serve holy God,*Acts 17:25*

Who made ev'rything on heaven and earth

And lives not in what puny thing man makes,*Acts 17:24*

Our God 'stead above all, over, supreme,*Ro 1:20*

    Beyond, outside, before, after, ahead,*Ro 11:34*

Day like a thousand years, thousand years day,*2Pe 3:8*

    Changing his course but not his character,*Jas 1:17*

Deepest deep, roaring waterfall, over you,*Psa 42:7*

    His glory looking to Israelite like

Consuming fire on clouded mountaintop,*Ex 24:17*

    Spectacular, inestimable God,*Ro 11:33*

Flames of fire serving him, carrying call,*Heb 1:7*

    Man's wisdom only utter foolishness,*1Co 1:25*

Making golden calf to worship, even

    As God gives Moses their own nation's laws,*Ex 32:4*

Jonah showing more concern sun shelter

    Than saving hundred-thousand Ninevites,*Jonah 4:10*

Balaam's donkey wiser than the prophet

    Who cannot see God's avenging angel,*Num 22:25*

Like the great fish that would obey God to

    Vomit Jonah from deep onto dry shore,*Jonah 2:10*

Wisdom not on earth among the living,*Job 28:13*

    But through God, who makes way for man to it:*Job 28:23*

Fear the Lord is wisdom, and to shun evil,*Job 28:28*

    For wisdom is open, calling from square,*Prov 1:20*

Crying from rooftops, speaking city gate;*Prov 1:21*

    Your duty, fear God, keep his commandments,*Ecc 12:13*

Trust in Lord, leaning not on your own standing,*Prov 3:5*

    But submit all ways, for him to direct.*Prov 3:6*

So God calls who contend with him to brace

Themselves against his storm, to answer him,*Job 40:6*

Because having no justice to condemn,*Job 40:8*

Having arms too short with him to contend.*Job 40:9*

Not you but he made the leviathan,*Job 41:1*

Not you but he made lurking behemoth,*Job 40:15*

That we like Joshua should fall facedown

In rev'rence, when appears his commander,*Joshua 5:14*

Our battles he to fight and win for him,

By trumpet call, Jer'cho walls tumbling down.*Joshua 6:5*

That we like Job should despise ourselves and

Prompt repent in ash having heard from him,*Job 42:6*

Making a cross! wiser than man's wisdom.*1Co 1:18*

Think about his true, noble, right, pure things,

Lovely, admirable, excellent things,*Php 4:8*

Practicing whatever you learn or hear,*Php 4:9*

For the noble make noble plans, and by

Noble deeds, they will be able to stand,*Isa 32:8*

The Son your wisdom from your wise Father,*1Co 1:30*

Declaring Father's myst'ry before time,*1Co 2:7*

That which rulers missed unwise, killing Son,*1Co 2:8*

You 'stead shrewd but innocent of blood.*Matt 10:16*

While his good news hides from the worldly wise,*Matt 11:25*

You rely, greater than fad, fashion, fancy,*1Th 5:24*

Father lav'shing love as best father,*1Jn 3:1*

Supreme and perfect, yours perfect Spirit.*Heb 12:23*

Hallowed, holy, honored, immense, potent,

Train of robe so vast as to fill temple,*Isa 6:1*

Seraphim covering faces and feet,*Isa 6:2*

    While calling holy, holy, holy God,*Isa 6:3*

That on sight, prophet would cry o'er unclean

    Lips, 'til seraphim tongs touched coal to mouth,*Isa 6:5*

Shaking smoke-hid stone doorposts and thresholds,*Isa 6:4*

    Yet no one sees Father but those who see Son,*1Ti 6:15*

Held in absolute awe, consumed in love,*Heb 12:28*

    None greater, only him, consequential,

As God protected Moses in rock's cleft

    To witness God's glory pass briefly by.*Exo 33:22*

Ev'rything disappears 'cept what Son said,*Matt 24:35*

    What the Son said, Father having said first,*Jn 14:10*

As ancient writings of Son's offer show,*Jn 5:39*

    Writings saying Father sent Son as own,*Jn 10:34-36*

Son doing then as ancient writings said,*Heb 10:7*

    His story ev'rywhere, ev'ryone told,*Ro 10:18*

Words forever free, you not always so,*2Ti 2:9*

    But you letting people also read you.*2Co 3:3*

Book 3: Coming

Ancestry

To accomplish your rescue, the Father

    Had to choose a people to bear his Son,*Ro 1:3*

Fitting royal line from which to issue

    Fourteen gen'rations Abra'm to David,

Fourteen more from David to the exile

    And another fourteen to royal Son,*Matt 1:1*

A people Israel, theirs the patriarchs,

    Tracing Messiah's human ancestry,*Ro 9:5*

But yet priest from indestructible life,*Heb 7:16*

    Still given royal human ancestry,

Lest his Son's coming appear sorcery,

    Magic, myth, or legend unfitting King

Of kings whose lineage traced to Adam,*Lk 3:23*

    Though Son came from God the Father only,

Not earthly father, but hist'ry records,

    The Father choosing unmarried Mary,

Spirit to carry to her unborn Son,*Matt 1:18*

    While 'ssuaging Joseph, her husband-to-be,

Dream messenger saying to trust Spirit,Matt 1:20

    That Mary bore the Father's Son Jesus,

Named for the rescue the Son would endure,

    Great light freeing of enslaving darkness.Matt 1:21

Micah Bethlehem Ephrathah foretold,Micah 5:2

    For most-royal birth, far home Galilee,

So Caesar census decreed to return

    Joseph to his ancestral Bethlehem,Lk 2:1

That all occur to convincing order,

    Joseph taking pregnant bride that the Son

Would issue from royal line of David,Lk 2:4

    That more know the Son's predicted mission.

Full confidence you should have in this work,

    Though Satan tempt you hist'ry to reject,1Th 3:5

Tempted loving money,1Ti 6:10 gospel to lose,2Th 3:2

    When instead you should trust the Son's good news,Ro 10:8

To look, see! There on the mountains, the feet

    Of one who brings good news, proclaiming peace,Nahum 1:15

Relieving you from having broken rules,Ro 2:28

    That the gospel does nonetheless respect,Ro 2:31

Restraining broken man, call to Savior,

    Human line, him to your temptation bear,

His coming, history's hinge, changing course

    From death to life, hope eternal in Son,

Like Jeremiah, condemned for exile,

    Buying Hanamel's field, deed in clay jar,Jer 32:6

In hope of release from captivity,

For restoration to Lord's promised land.*Jer 33:7*

Incarnation

Micah right: Mary bore Bethlehem Son,*Micah 5:2*

    Though come not as powerful dictator,

Like many kings Israel begged Samuel rule,*1Samuel 8:5*

    Kings so hard, Israel cried out for relief,*1Samuel 8:18*

How long, Lord, must we call for help when you

    Do not listen, plead, but you do not save?*Hab 1:2*

Nor tall and handsome, appearance as judge,

    When Lord instead looks sole at David's heart,*1Samuel 16:7*

So helpless newborn, like any of us,

    Wrapped in cloths as any mother would do,*Lk 2:7*

No room in town of census visitors

    For man's King, except in low livestock pen,*Lk 2:6*

Son coming humbly, inn'cent, vulner'ble,

    Precar'ous, as we live needing rescue,*Deut 28:29*

As Abr'am rescued captured Lot from kings,*Gen 14:14*

    And Reuben rescued brother Joseph's life.*Gen 37:21*

Son's coming warranted announcement grand,

    Father sending shepherds night messenger,

Near Bethlehem flocks, brilliant light shining,*Lk 2:8*

    Saying not to fear but good news rejoice,

Savior has come as newborn infant,

    Surprise to find wrapped in livestock manger.*Lk 2:10*

Angel cloud instant 'ppeared, shout glory God!

    Promising peace on earth in his favor.*Lk 2:13*

Shepherds ran for manger near, where Mary

    Tended world-ruler Son as swaddled babe,*Lk 2:15*

Then spreading 'mazed word to honor Father,

    Newborn Savior they had seen, angel told,*Lk 2:17*

Mary in her heart wonders to ponder,*Lk 2:19*

    To bear a Son of truth and compassion,*Jn 1:14*

Good news readied for you 'fore time began,*2Ti 1:9*

    As Isaiah also foretold, virgin

Conceiving to bear son Immanuel,*Isa 7:14*

    Meaning God with us, living among us,*Matt 1:23*

Pure gift from Father above, out of love,

    Not as you deserved,*Ro 1:5* not as you have earned,*Gal 2:21*

Just so Father may pour his love on you

    Because of his love for his only Son,*1Ti 1:14*

God with us, when not with us disaster

    And calamity reign, Savior absent,*Deut 31:17*

Just as en'my perish when God with them,

    As befell Ashdod, with Dagon their god,

Ark of the one true God then to return.*1Sam 5:7*

    So God be with us as our ancestors,*1Kings 8:57*

Never leave nor forsake us, but abide,

    That to God's house we may go, shouting joy,*Ro 42:4*

And that God accompany our armies,*Psa 108:11*

    Defeat evil strategy, protecting,*Isa 8:10*

That nations follow, holding hem of robe,*Zech 8:23*

    Having heard and seen that God is with you.

Presentation

The world now had its infant Rescuer,

    Circumcised at eighth day, Jesus named,

As angel messenger had instructed,

    Following God of order, law observed,*Lk 2:21*

Even taking Son to Jerusalem,

    Parents sacrifice made to retrieve Son,*Lk 2:22*

First-born ritual honoring the Father,

    Remembering exodus from Egypt,*Heb 11:22*

While foreshadowing Father's gift of Son,

    All setting apart his chosen people.*Deut 7:6*

To show the Son no ordinary babe,

    Sincere Simeon, who had waited long

To see Israel's savior,*Lk 2:25* met Son's parents

    In temple courtyards, Sim'on die in peace,

For seeing the Savior of all people,*Lk 2:27*

    While he also warned of great upheaval.*Lk 2:33*

Mary and Joseph marveled at such words,

    More when widow Anna, fasting, praying

Contin'ally to see Savior, said same,*Lk 2:38*

    Father announcing Christ through his prophets,

Son whom Father gave power before time,*Jude 24*

    Power forever,*1Pe 4:11* to sustain all things,*Heb 1:3*

Son shown in blazing fire angels attend,*2Th 1:7*

    Son over every other power,*Col 2:10*

Living by Father's unlimited power,*2Co 13:4*

    Simple power, not fancy philos'phy,*1Co 1:17*

43

As heaven rejoiced at the Son's coming,

    Having eons waited for promised day.

Announcement

The Son's coming drew far wider notice

    Than shepherds and sincerely devoted,

For Eastern sages knew sacred writings,

    Watching for star 'nnouncing Son's arrival,*Matt 2:1*

To travel far to capitol city,

    There to ask to worship the One just come.*Matt 2:2*

Their arrival roiled Jerusalem,*Matt 2:3*

    Where all knew messianic prediction,

But wicked Herod 'gainst iron rule,

    Who called to learn where Savior would come,*Matt 2:4*

In Bethlehem, of course, where monarch must

    Plot how to kill the now-come King of kings,*Matt 2:4*

Whose parents hid him, as Jehosheba

    Hid infant king Joash in the Temple,*2Kings 11:2*

Levite woman hid her fine child Moses,*Exo 2:1*

    'Til papyrus basket bore Pharaoh's child.*Exo 2:3*

Meanwhile, star led sages to young child King,*Matt 2:9*

    There to bow in worship true, prostrate fell,

Treasures borne royalty gold, divine oil

    Of Spirit told, and resin burial

Foreseen, sages encountered the young King,*Matt 2:11*

    Virgin indeed bearing the Son whom all

Would know as God with us, Immanuel,

Father come in the person of the Son.*Matt 1:22*

Wicked monarch was not done, Joseph learned,

    Dream warning to take Mary and young Son

To Egypt 'til Herod died, once again

    To fulfill ancient prophesy,*Hosea 11:1* Father

To call his Son out of Egypt's slav'ry,*Matt 2:13*

    Out of Egypt, out of slav'ry must come,

As God drew Moses,*Exo 2:10* to draw out Israel,

    After Herod had killed Bethlehem's young,

In prophesy that region's mothers weep,*Jer 31:15*

    Over their lost children,*Jer 31:15* everything as

Ancient writings said,*Matt 2:16* even when Joseph

    Brought his family back to Nazareth,

Avoiding wicked monarch's reigning son,

    So anointed Christ would Nazarene be,*Matt 2:22*

For no word the Lord speaks fails of purpose,*2Kings 10:10*

    The Lord announcing things before they spring,*Isa 42:9*

As he announced Nebuchadnezzar's craze,*Dan 4:17*

    Even announced the good news to Abraham,*Gal 3:8*

That you know him sov'reign and cannot say

    Your wooden and metal gods brought them 'bout.*Isa 48:5*

God came not that you stay the same but change,

    Life forever leaving you no regrets,*2Co 7:10*

Your conscience eager that change defend you,*2Co 7:11*

    Admitting wrong,*Jas 5:16* not stubborn,*Ro 2:5* not corrupt,*Jas 4:8*

But turned from those things that others indulge,*2Co 12:21*

    To be like the Father whom you now know,*1Pe 1:14*

Relying on Son, your Father to show,*Acts 20:21*

    The Father's place so very close to you,*Matt 4:17*

His celest'al beings to celebrate

    When so few as one of you turns to him,*Lk 15:8*

As he waits patiently for your heart seek,

    So you do not die but live in the Son.*2Pe 3:9*

Maturation

Young Son had to grow as any man would,

    Mature, strong, as Nazareth carpenter,*Lk 2:39*

Like Samson whom the Lord's Spirit stirred as

    He grew to maturity, his day come,*Jdg 13:25*

Or David's Solomon, Bathsheba's son,

    Whom the Lord favored to build his temple,*2Sam 12:24*

Or Jacob's son Joseph whom his father loved,

    Per'lously, more than his other children,*Gen 37:3*

Or Moses' brave aide since youth, Joshua,

    Who by his leader stood, lone to survive,*Num 14:38*

The Father's favor and poise evident,*Lk 2:40*

    As when Joseph and Mary to Jerusalem

Returned for Passover festival,*Lk 2:41* and

    Son, though twelve, remained,*Lk 2:42* scholars to debate,*Lk 2:45*

Amazing ev'ryone with what he knew,*Lk 2:47*

    His parents 'stonished why Son had let them search,*Lk 2:48*

But should know he was in his Father's house,*Lk 2:49*

    Prompt to return to Nazareth good Son,

To grow strong in stature and deep in wisdom,*Lk 2:51*

While Mary's heart treasured these special things,*Lk 2:52*

'Til at thirty Son's mission public came,*Lk 3:23*

The Father perfect entry granted Son.

Now for this Son of Man, do as he says,*Jn 14:15*

Father loving whoever obeys Son,*Jn 14:23*

Like Jonah obeyed God to go preach to

The great wicked city of Nineveh,*Jonah 3:3*

Those not obeying not loving the Son,*Jn 14:24*

Son's friend only if you do as he says,*Jn 15:14*

Being consistent, not contradict'ry,*2Co 1:18*

As prophet Nathan showed David he was,

Stealing Uriah's ewe lamb Bathsheba,*2Samuel 12:4*

Doing the good that others should expect,*1Ti 6:20*

Not compromising, as Israelites did,

Taking part of promised land, angel Lord

Rebuking them straight from Gilgal at Bokim,*Jdg 2:1*

Or as Saul did, sparing Agag and best sheep,*1Samuel 15:9*

Samuel bleating hear,*1Samuel 15:14* Lord rejecting king,*1Samuel 15:26*

Or as one turns away from godly due,

To say thing owed is Corban, God devoted,*Mk 7:11*

But 'stead be full obedient to God.

Nature

This coming the Son's nature established,

Without beginning or end because with

Father before they spoke and time began,*Heb 7:1*

God Almighty who brought forth the Savior,*Heb 1:5*

47

So that even angels would worship him,*Heb 1:6*

    And transcendent living would then begin.*Col 1:18*

While you may think angels extraord'nary,

    Son is far super'or 'cause from Father,*Heb 1:4*

No lesser being would do than from him,*Heb 4:14*

    Father's sacred Spirit devoted Son,*Ro 1:4*

Son pleasing Father, Father loving Son,*2Pe 1:17*

    Son kind and loving Savior, come for you.*Tit 3:3-5*

Son too made invis'ble Father vis'ble,

    Father's image, no longer imagined,*Col 1:15*

Son radiating the Father's grandeur,

    Exactly representing his being,*Heb 1:3*

The Father's fullness, supernat'ral self,

    Made plain for you, e'en to touch, hear, and see,*Col 2:9*

Wonder nothing distasteful for Father,

    Who loves living and breathing in the Son,*Col 1:19*

As he invites you live and breathe in him,*1Jn 5:20*

    Knowing just who came to you incarnate.

So know with Son come that your rule keeping

    Matters naught but to rely on good news,*Gal 3:5*

Welcoming Spirit's life-giving freedom,*Ro 8:2*

    Jubilee year, released to return home,

Freed to enter the Lord's blessed service,*Lev 25:54*

    Cleaned,*Ro 10:4* restored to order, Son healed and cured,*Gal 3:21*

Free again,*Gal 3:23* Spirit influenced, turned to

    The Father's desires as the Son shows you.*Ro 8:3-4*

Wonderful Counselor, Almighty God,

Everlasting Father, your Prince of Peace,*Isa 9:6*

Though infant born, presented, announced, raised,

And matured, the Son is God among us,

Being in very nature God, yet not

Counting that nature to his advantage.*Php 2:6*

Book 4: Immersion

Messenger

Though on incarnation history hinged,

 Immanuel wondrously among us,

Preparation remained, Son's immersion

 Into new birth and to receive Spirit,

Introduction, induction, signify

 Profound events to come in witness Son.

Priest Zechariah and good wife 'Liz'beth,

 Noble character worth more than rubies,*Prov 31:10*

Her husband his full confidence in her,*Prov 31:11*

 Though virtuous, had grown old with no child,*Lk 1:5*

But annual draw called Zechariah

 To enter the inner Temple, incense

To burn for the people's holy prayers,*Lk 1:8*

 So when Zechariah entered, awesome

Angel confronted him, expecting death,*Lk 1:11*

 But 'stead fear not, said holy messenger

Father's word conveyed that 'Liz'beth child bear,

 To name John,*Lk 1:13* to delight them and others,

Because great in the Father's sight, never

Drinking wine, pure for the Spirit to fill._Lk 1:14_

John would call many back to the Father,

Like the miracle-working Elijah,

Turning parents' hearts back to their children,_Mal 4:6_

Those doing wrong turned to again do right,

Most, though, to prepare for the Father's Son,

John the Baptist, the Son's special herald._Lk 1:16_

Zechariah asked fearsome angel, though,

How he could be sure, mute he then 'til birth,_Lk 1:18_

In consequence the angel disbelieve,_Lk 1:21_

When all would pass as said, 'Liz'beth conceived,_Lk 1:23_

Pregnant Mary vis'ting cousin 'Liz'beth,

in whose womb John lept, hearing Mary's voice,

Mother of his coming Lord to baptize,_Lk 1:39_

Spirit filling 'Liz'beth who blessed Mary,

As mother of her own coming Savior,_Lk 1:41_

Mary blessing the Father in own song._Lk 1:46_

So the Baptist came like the Son himself,

With angel messenger foretelling role,

Ours to obey Father's word, lest we, like

Zechariah, our voice lose to his scorn,

Instead to honor rulers God installs,_1Pe 2:17_

Doing so even for your harsh employer,_1Pe 2:18_

So that no one slanders the Father for you,_1Ti 6:1_

Serving better those, on Son relying,_1Ti 6:2_

While sharing good news for others to obey,_Ro 1:5_

Giving Caesar government its own due._Mk 12:13_

Message

John was not light but witness to Son's light,*Jn 1:6*

    That all would know what the Son's coming meant,

'Liz'beth, as angel said, naming child John,*Lk 1:57*

    Still-mute Zechariah writing the same,*Lk 1:61*

Spirit filled, then prophesying honor,

    that John would way prepare for Father's Son,*Lk 1:67*

News of John then to spread, with wonder that

    Father so clearly touched priest's Baptist son.*Lk 1:65*

Living in wilderness, John's spirit grew,*Lk 1:80*

    Eating no bread, drinking no wine, strong, pure,

But to people seeming demon possessed,*Lk 7:33*

    Doing exactly as angel had said,

Preparing the way for the Son his Lord,*Mk 1:2*

    Calling the people to repent of sin,

Because the Son was bringing his good news.*Mk 1:3*

    Covered by camel skin held by plain belt,

Baptist ate only locusts and honey,

    Saying one more powerful was to come,*Mk 1:6*

Who, though after John, would supersede John,

    Because Son was before and above John,*Jn 1:15*

Who could save none but only make Son's way,

    Set straight for Son in Israel wilderness.*Jn 1:19-23*

The Son later said that none naturally born

    Is greater than this last greatest prophet,

But least under Son is greater than John,*Matt 11:11*

    Whom they had pursued because God's prophet,*Matt 11:7*

None believing Son but believing John,

    When he the Son's good news was declaring,*Jn 5:31-32*

Except the priests and officials refused

    Even John to believe, never to change,*Matt 21:32*

Though their ancient writings did John foretell,*Matt 11:14*

    As Isaiah predicted Son's honor,*Jn 12:41*

Prophet Isaiah whose name means God saves,

    Son Shear-Jashub means remnant returns.

Honor, the Son did not seek but Father wrought,*Jn 8:50*

    Son's obedience honoring Father,*Jn 12:27*

As prophets searched to discover when and how

    Son would come, suffer, and receive honor,*1Pe 1:10*

That the Father shared with Son before time,*Jn 17:4*

    As Son honors those who rely on him.*Jn 17:22*

Immersing

John had other role beyond Son's herald,

    To immerse, enjoin, initiate, and

Induct the people, that they change their ways,

    To draw to Jordan River wilderness,

To tell how in the Son they could go free,*Lk 3:1*

    Isaiah wrote, wilderness voice calling,*Isa 40:3*

The people to prepare for their rescue,*Lk 3:4*

    Baptist immersing the willing, drowning

Their corruption in Jordan River flow,*Matt 3:4*

   As God cleansed with the great flood save Noah,*Gen 6:17*

Never again to destroy all life in flood,*Gen 9:11*

   Only God's ark-borne word holding back flood,

As Joshua led nation 'cross Jordan,*Joshua 4:18*

   On way to occupying promised land,

The Father's next open floodgate blessing,

   Pouring out so much, no room to store it,*Mal 3:10*

Prosperous, numerous, hearts open, home,

   Blessings he promised for turning to Lord.*Deut 30:5*

But Baptist John came like pent floodwaters,

   The Lord's breath driving his fir'y preaching,*Isa 59:19*

Wretched, pitiful crowds flocking to him,

   Broods of vipers he called them,*Lk 3:7* judgment come,

Brought low to ground, voices only ghostlike,

   Heard out of the dust, barely a whisper,*Isa 29:4*

To cut for firewood like fruitless trees,*Lk 3:8*

   Unworthy of so great and holy Lord,

Yet demons drowned in the Baptist's dunking,*Mk 1:5*

   To stop cheating, extorting, and hoarding,*Lk 3:10*

But heed God's offer of life over death,

   In your loving walk, obeying the Lord.*Deut 30:15*

The Father's baptism cleanses, prepares,

   Making you better in every way,*1Co 1:5*

To join the Father, relying on Son,*Heb 10:22*

   Proven perfect through awful suffering,*Heb 2:10*

Immersion cleaning you all the way through,*1Th 5:23*

The Spirit's cleansing work rescuing you,*2Th 2:13*

So Father can reward the pure in heart,*Matt 5:8*

Son making you perfect, like Father,*Matt 5:48*

Conscience clear, freed of death, serving Father,*Heb 9:14*

The Son's obed'ence making you blameless.*Ro 5:19*

Not all submitted to baptism, John

Condemning the priests who relied on their

Supposed pure person and ancestry,*Matt 3:7*

Whose parents 'stead raised stone-stupid children,*Matt3:9*

As John warned, Father ready to chop down

Who refused the holy Baptist's cleansing,*Matt 3:10*

Like Jehu killed Baal's prophets and Ahab's line

To destroy false worship in all Israel.*2Kings 10:28*

Final induction would come when Son doused

With the Father's fire, his Holy Spirit,*Lk 3:16*

John introducing greater immersion,*Mk 1:8*

When Spirit would descend in holy flames,*Acts 1:4*

From Son who was already among them,*Jn 1:24*

John already witness to coming Son.*Lk 3:18*

Descent

Strong and mature Son finally came to John,

For own Jordan-wilderness immersion,*Mk 1:9*

John knowing the moment immed'ately,

On Son's first far-off approach, the One come,

Baptist told the crowd, to assuage all wrong,

Greater than Baptist, John's glad admission,*Jn 1:29*

Humbly asking that the Son immerse him!*Matt 3:14*

But Son fast corrected John immerse Son,

The Father having ordered things that way,

His plan theirs sure to keep to perfection.*Matt 3:15*

Baptist swift immersed Son wholly under,*Lk 3:21*

Son needing no cleanse, only induction,

Calling to his Father at moment grand,

Father glad to answer, opening heaven,*Lk 3:21*

Not to release bright beam, awesome dragon,

But Spirit, gently fluttered,*Isa 42:1* pure love to

Alight on perfect Son's plain human form,

No beauty or majesty attracting,

No appearance to make us desire him,*Isa 53:2*

As Son rose from water to welcome him,*Matt 3:16*

John vocal witness to the Spirit's descent,*Jn 1:32*

As Son himself later said, to baptize

In name of the Father, Son, and Spirit,*Matt 28:18*

To know that John would see Spirit descend,

As Father's angel had also said Son

Would baptize with Father's Holy Spirit,*Jn 1:33*

Shoot from Jesse's stump, Lord's Branch,*Isa 11:1* receiving

Lord's Spirit of wisdom, understanding,

Counsel, might, and knowledge, fear of the Lord,*Isa 11:2*

Sevenfold spirits of God whom Christ holds.*Rev 3:1*

These truths Father's own voice spoke at baptism,

That Son had pleased Father whom Father loved,

Those witnesses present all agreeing,*Matt 3:17*

    Father confirmed, the Son his to honor.*2Pe 1:17*

Son thus asks Father send Spirit helper,*Jn 14:15*

    Advocate to remind you ev'rything,*Jn 14:25*

Correcting what naturally condemns,*Jn 16:8*

    Revealing what Spirit learns from the Son,*Jn 16:14*

Through whom you know Father sent your Savior,*1Jn 4:13*

    Knowing Son only when having Spirit,*Ro 8:9*

Spirit bringing you back to life, perfect,*Ro 8:10*

    As Father's will that you be his Son's own,*Ro 8:16*

Listening to Spirit's advocacy,*Ro 8:27*

    Knowing you love Son only with Spirit,*1Co 12:3*

Son's sacrifice pouring out the Spirit,*Tit 5:6*

    As prophet Joel said, old men dreaming,

Young men seeing visions, sons and daughters

    Prophesying, Spirit poured out on all,*Joel 2:28*

Afterward, in last days, day of the Lord,*Acts 2:17*

    When Father is Spirit, yours in embrace.*2Co 3:17*

Passage

Thus ended passage from prophets of old,

    To new life in the Son, as John next day

Told crowd to see pass by the gentle One

    Whom men would soon brutally sacrifice,*Jn 1:35*

This passage obv'ous when later John, in

    Prison for truth spoken tetrarch Herod,

Hearing of Son's ministry, sent students

    To confirm Son was Father's chosen one,*Matt 11:2*

And Son cited wonders seen ev'ryone,

    That the blind saw, lame walked, sick healed, deaf heard,

Even dead lived again, the good news heard,*Lk 7:21*

    Some confused, thinking Son prophet or John,

Peter though saying Son was chosen One,*Mk 7:27*

    In great passage like of old when Moses

Laid hand of leadership on aide Joshua,*Num 27:18*

    To conquer, inhabit the promised land,

When others feared looking like grasshoppers

    In mighty occupying natives' sight,*Num 13:28*

Or David son Solomon anointed,*1Kings 1:17*

    Lest many kingdom enemies prevail.

Herod then John's head on platter bore,*Mk 6:21*

    Though Herod liked to hear John Baptist roar,

In reward for Herod'as daughter's dance,

    His word to keep,*Matt 14:3* though John innocent was,

Herod'as' grudge nursed to bitter effect,*Mk 6:17*

    Tetrarch's birthday spoils, seduced to murder.*Mk 6:21-28*

Though evil meant, passage was now complete,

    Son on with work that Baptist John forecast,

Tetrarch hearing Son's wonders from John passed,*Mk 6:14*

    Thinking 'Lijah or other seer back,*Lk 9:7-9*

When Son honored John as last great prophet,

    Though Son would also suffer prophet's fate.*Mk 9:11*

Late in his earthly service, Son returned

To Jordan place where John the Son immersed,

Many joining Son to say John was right,

Winning many more to their Savior come, *Jn 10:40*

Son's immersion thus fully effective, *Lk 12:50*

Awful immersion—tort'rous murder!—still.

Son trusted Father, *Heb 3:2* who put Son o'er you, *Heb 3:6*

To rely on Son's vict'ry as your own. *Heb 6:19*

Persistence

These immersions into faith and spirit

Continued, e'en after Son died and rose,

Bringing the new life that truth affords, in

That great moment when Father sent Spirit

To Pentecost Jerusalem crowd, when

Peter and apostles baptized thousands, *Acts 2:39*

While Philip many Samarian more,

All with the Spirit welcoming good news,

E'en Simon sorcerer whom Philip's signs

so greatly astonished, *Acts 8:13* and Ethiop'an

Eunuch who chariot stopped to immerse, *Acts 8:36*

After reading Isaiah telling Son,

Even Roman commander and family

Accepting Peter's good-news baptism,

Kind-hearted soldier also winning friends

To the Lord's side, *Acts 10:44* Spirit likewise op'ning

Cloth seller Lydia's heart, Paul baptized

Her whole household to welcome the Spirit,*Acts 16:13*

Even jailer and household Paul baptized

When earthquake opened prison to good news.*Acts 16:25*

Opposition only spreads the good news,

Always free, carrying its immersion,

As when Corinth synagogue opposed Paul,

Who went next door to Titius Justus,

Carrying there the Lord's gospel message,

So Paul baptized many Corinthians;*Acts 18:5*

Even magicians Jannes and Jambres

Opposed Moses,*2Tim 3:8* as one expects with

Sharing the truth, that opposition will

Always arise from the Lord's enemy.

But these immersions continue today

And will until the Lord's welcome return,

So that you may share in the Son's honor,*2Th 2:14*

Like the Father's children you also

Are when suffering with the Father's Son,*Ro 8:16-17*

Though your suffering could never compare

With the honor the Father will show you,*Ro 8:18*

The good news your whole hope for his honor.*Col 1:27*

Effect

Baptism's effect was glorious for

Those faithful who welcomed and received it,

Marking passage into the Son's new life,

Even as foolish officials refused,*Lk 7:29*

Its good effect not from the old Baptist

But from Son to whom baptism pointed.*Jn 3:22*

Baptism burying your sin hist'ry,

Permanently, as old self dies with Son,

So that the Father can lift you again

As Father did his Son in whom you died,*Ro 6:3*

Your faith in Father's plan releasing

The Father's power through the Son's service,*Col 2:12*

Just as you have power to excuse wrongs,*Jn 20:23*

As often as must, not even counting,*Matt 18:21*

No census take,*Num 1:2* no transgressions number,

No offenses nurture, all forgiven,

Like God excused you, you better others,*Matt 18:23*

Father treating you as you treat others,*Matt 6:14*

Otherwise, the enemy getting you all.*2Co 2:10*

So better excuse those who abandon,*2Ti 4:16*

Lest they fall to pieces from your punishment,*2Co 2:6*

Asking instead that Father excuse them,*Jas 5:13*

While not dealing with those who hold grudges,*2Ti 3:2*

Instead putting on Son as your clothing.*Gal 3:27*

Baptism is not physical cleaning

But conscience cleansing, correcting your act,

Not just for your neighbor but your Father,*1Pe 3:21*

Your immersion with the Father's own Son,*1Co 1:11*

The old way having tremendous honor,

But the Son's new way far greater honor.*2Co 3:7*

Lasting, as salvation does, forever;*2Co 3:11*

    In baptism, to Father and Son look,*2Co 3:18*

Your sole deliverance from Mount Zion,*Oba 17*

    Fire Jacob to inherit, Joseph flame.*Oba 18*

Then look beyond to your fire dousing

    With the Father's own refining Spirit,

As Apollos, knowing water Baptism,

    learned from Aquila and wife Priscilla,*Acts 18:25*

And Paul taught the John-baptized Ephesians

    Also to receive Spirit baptism,*Acts 19:1*

So that when he touched them, they spoke other

    Languages, and they also prophesied,*Acts 19:6*

As Saul had prophesied among prophets,*1Sam 10:10*

    When Samuel anointed with Spirit's oil,

Again Saul prophesied when God's Spirit

    Descended as he traveled to Naioth.*1Samuel 19:23*

All believers draw from the same Spirit,*1Co 12:13*

    As all believers rely on the Son's

Resurrection, his coming back to life,

    To give immersion its meaning,*1Co 15:29*

Adam turning away from the Father

    Who made him, but perfect Son not turning,*Ro 5:14*

Instead immersing in needless cleansing,

    Then to bleed in own willing sacrifice,*1Jn 5:6*

Named Jesus as your literal rescue,*Matt 1:21*

    Freeing you from death if you accept him,*Jn 4:39*

Bringing together all, no matter place,*Jn 11:49*

Son how to live with creator Father.*Jn 14:4*

Son as Father's substance in human form,

Relinquished to die as your rescuer,*Php 2:6*

Accepting Son to embrace what Father

Said about him, not a liar to make,*1Jn 5:10*

But gift for ev'ryone,*Heb 2:9* far better than

Sacrificing your brothers and sisters.*Heb 12:24*

Tempting

Baptism brings conscience, that wonderful voice

Of the Father's Spirit, to resist harm,

As our Lord showed when after baptism

the Spirit led him into wilderness

For forty days of testing, confirming

Spirit presence and power to protect,*Mk 1:12*

'Gainst ev'ry temptation, hunger and thirst,*Lk 4:1*

To survive sole on Spirit sustenance,*Matt 4:2*

The Father's angels attending the Son,*Mk 1:13*

That Spirit-fed in desert he may thrive,

And not temptation fall as David fell

When sight of bathing Bathsheba eye caught,*2Sam 11:2*

King should war been,*2Sam 11:1* husband Uriah,

Hittite murder betray, lost to lust,*2Sam 11:17*

As Amnon obsessed over beautiful

Sister Tamar,*2Sam 13:2* to rape her,*2Sam 13:14* and die,*2Sam 13:29*

Or spying red stew, famished Esau his

Birthright to sell Jacob, e'er to despise,*Gen 25:33*

So to marry Hittite women, parents

Grieved,*Gen 26:34* losing blessing to trickster brother,*Gen27:34*

Deceiver whom father-in-law Laban

Would soon deceive into taking second

Wife of weak eyes over lovely formed first,*Gen 29:25*

Who must children buy with her son's mandrakes,*Gen 30:15*

Jacob to return Laban peeled-poplar

Branch deception to earn more-than-due wage,*Gen 30:37*

Rachel even stealing father Laban's

Household gods, period hid under saddle,*Gen 31:34*

Sons Simeon and Levi deceive and

Slaughter Shechemites o'er Dinah's defile,*Gen 34:13*

Man sure to deceive Satan-deceived man,

Adam-inclined from birth, selfish evil.

See, the Son's straight truth truly sets you free,*Jn 8:31*

So that you are free indeed of all need,*Jn 8:36*

Able resist temptation as Joseph

Entreat resisted of Potiphar's wife,*Gen 39:8*

Made for freedom, not to indulge but serve,*Gal 5:13*

Doing ev'rything required, when loving

Neighbor as self,*Gal 5:14* free of sin's wrongdoing,*1Pe 2:16*

No one condemning because Son has you,*Ro 8:34*

No worries,*Php 4:6* no needs, instead satisfied,*Php 4:11*

Neither a lot nor little mattering,*Php 4:12*

The Father meeting all your genuine needs,*Php 4:19*

Always free because obeying the Son.*1Co 7:22*

At forty day's end, the adversary

>Tempted sore the Son at weakest moment,

With God's power Son could turn stones to bread,*Matt 4:3*

>Strongest appeal to Father's own power,

Though Son respond that man, yes man, though here

>Son of Man, live on Father's word alone,*Lk 4:4*

Adversary to try other appeal,

>Having Son stand on Temple pinnacle,

To jump for angels catch, quoth enemy,*Matt 4:6*

>Though Son quote back to the adversary,

The Father not to test 'gainst his own words,*Lk 4:12*

>Here to see Son doing as we all should,

Maturing under trial, using word

>As God intended,*Ro 6:1* refusing quarter,*Ro 6:13*

Nothing holding sway over whom Son freed,*Ro 6:14*

>Prepared to resist to remain so free,*1Co 6:12*

Following Father's desires than one's own,*1Co 15:34*

>Father's power turning you from all wrong.*2Co 13:4*

Adversary then to mountaintop took

>Son to see every worldly splendor,

Offering Son all for obed'ent bow,*Lk 4:5*

>Son instead quote to serve Father only,*Matt 4:10*

As perseverance works, adversary flee,

>Father's angels then Son again attend,*Matt 4:11*

'Til adversary sense better trial,*Lk 4:13*

>Sure to come, to no avail 'gainst the Son.

So we walk in Son's words rather than blind,*Acts 13:6*

Letting no hint of unrestraint compel_Eph 5:3_

Like Eli's sons, forks deep in offering, _1Samuel 3:13_

Obscenity, foolish talk, coarse joking,_Eph 5:4_

Cursed, stupid, dumber than an animal,_1Pe 2:14_

Storm-driven along to their own deep pit._1Pe 2:17_

Book 5: Mission

Announcing

Life should have mission and purpose, shape, form,

    As Abra'm God called to father nation,*Neh 9:7*

Moses called to give same nation freedom,*Exo 3:8*

    Joshua to conquer the promised land,*Joshua 1:3*

Prostitute Rahab to hide Israel's spies,*Joshua 2:1*

    Heber's Jael to kill Sis'ra with tent peg,*Jdg 4:21*

Gideon to again free his people,*Jdg 6:12*

    David to follow God with all his heart,*1Kings 14:8*

Solomon to build the Father's temple,*1Kings 8:18*

    Elkanah's Hannah bear prophet Samuel,*1Sam 1:19*

Abigail suffer fool husband Nabal,*1Sam 25:3*

    Jonah to prophesy to Nineveh,*Jonah 1:2*

Grandmother Lois and mother Eunice

    To raise 'postle Paul's apprentice Timothy,*2Tim 1:5*

Each with purpose, as you have your purpose,

    Part of the greatest story ever told,

As the Son had his reason for coming,

    Legacy leave through Father's gospel plan,

Humanity to save from Adam's sin,

　　Good-news plan of which you are urgent heart,

For God knit you 'gether in mother's womb,

　　Created your inmost being,*Psa 139:13* making

You fearfully, wonderf'lly, as you know well,*Psa 139:14*

　　All your days God's book ordained, before first.*Psa 139:16*

The Son went to work after his baptism,

　　In showing the Father's door now open,

All who turn inherit as Father's child,*Matt 4:17*

　　As Son first proclaimed in his home region,*Mk 1:14*

From village to village, Son the good news,*Mk 1:38*

　　Spread quickly through familiar Galilee,*Mk 1:28*

People crowding 'round to hear Son's message,*Mk 2:1*

　　As he moved swiftly to reach ev'ry town,

On his Father's one great assigned mission,*Lk 4:43*

　　Twelve disciples accompanying him,

Women supporting the traveling band,*Lk 8:1*

　　Son commissioning those join him.*Mk 3:13*

So should we our talents use, news to spread,

　　Doing more than Son, as even Son said,*Jn 14:12*

Prophesying confident if given,*Ro 12:6*

　　Serving gen'rously if given instead,*Ro 12:7*

Teaching consistently if a teacher,*Ro 12:7*

　　Encouraging many if God so formed,*Ro 12:8*

Giving abundantly if so God blessed,*Ro 12:8*

　　Father accepting whate'er your talent,*1Co 12:5*

For to honor Lord with your firstfruit wealth,*Prov 3:9*

Is to fill your barns to overflowing,*Prov 3:10*

To bring your whole tithe for food in God's house

Tests God, throwing open heaven's floodgates.*Mal 3:10*

Teaching

The Son's good news was so profound as to

Require of Son that he be the Teacher,

As Laz'rus' sister Martha, fam'ly friend,

Disciples, and others called Lord Jesus,*Jn 11:28*

That he would give the good news its fullness,

Son affirming them, for Teacher he was,*Jn 13:13*

With Spirit authority and power,*Lk 4:14*

Teaching exactly what his message meant.*Matt 4:23*

We rightly hesitate to teach, Father

Judging teachers more strictly than others,*Jas 3:1*

Speaker training meaning nothing aside

From the Spirit-carried gospel message,*2Co 11:6*

Yet follow a sound teacher's example,

Surely when the teacher follows the Son,*1Co 11:1*

Imitating whose message you welcome,

Even as you also imitate Son,*1Th 1:6*

Not looking back to old ways like Lot's wife,

Turning to pillar of salt,*Gen 19:26* but forward,

So you, too, may model Son for others,*1Th 1:7*

Speaking good news to sensible people,*1Co 10:15*

For beautiful along mountain paths are

The feet of witnesses who bring good news,*Isa 52:7*

Able to teach,*2Ti 2:24* modeling the Teacher,*Lk 6:40*

Teaching others to do as the Son said,*Matt 28:18*

Reasoning wisely with those whom you teach,*Acts 18:19-21*

Patiently, carefully,*2Ti 4:2* not persuasion

But the Spirit's power,*1Co 2:4* openly, all

Good news that the Son secretly taught you.*Matt 10:27*

Teach to increase your hearer's confidence

In living forever,*Tit 1:1* not from envy,*Php 1:15-16*

But whatever motive, teach only the Son,*Php 1:18*

Diligently with your whole, improving,*1Ti 4:13*

Soundly,*2Th 2:15* only from the ancient writings,*Ro 15:4*

Speaking solely the Father's very words,*1Pe 4:11*

The Son's truth as your conscience confirms it,*Ro 9:1*

Consistent with what the Son himself says.*2Co 10:5*

Who teaches matters not, what's taught mattering, and

What's learned mattering more,*1Co 15:11* only good news.*2Ti 4:5*

The Son taught meaningful things, commanding,

Amazing with matters not before heard,*Lk 4:31*

So powerful, gaining such following,

Council member Nicodemus secret

Night visit he made to learn from the Son,*Jn 3:1*

Born again to hear, truth stupefied,*Jn 3:3*

As Jesus taught in ev'ry synagogue,

Unstoppable, over-turning good news,*Matt 9:35*

Always at work, as you should also work,

Finishing the Father's start, only value,*Matt 15:13*

Doing as the Father assigns, this, that,*1Co 3:5*

    Pleasing the Spirit who helps eternal,*Gal 6:8*

Working when you cannot see the result,*1Co 15:37*

    Sharing the good news that no one else will,*3Jn 7*

More done, more received,*2Co 9:6* reaping what one sows,*Gal 6:7*

    Spare if sparingly,*2Co 9:6* rich when gen'rous sown.

The Son's compassion for the crowds kept him

    teaching thoroughly and diligently,

The people harassed and helpless, their leaders

    Doing nothing for them, clueless, guessing,*Matt 9:36*

And so the Son taught in every town,

    Just the teaching that the crowds required,*Matt 11:1*

In boat off lakeshore when necessary,*Mk 4:1*

    Amazing even his hometown hearers,*Matt 13:53*

Nothing ord'nary, 'stead astonishing,

    Not with impertinence or foolishness

But with resonating truth, the message,*Matt 22:33*

    In high Jerusalem Temple courtyards,

To camp each evening on Olive Mount,*Lk 21:37*

    Relentless pace, disciples could not keep,

Warning that bad intent makes bad teaching,*Lk 6:45*

    To guard against wrong message, falsely taught,*Matt 16:5*

'Gainst teachers making students follow them

    Rather than pointing to God's holy Son,*Acts 20:30*

Teaching useless myths and speculation,*1Ti 1:3*

    Of meaningless if entertaining talk,*1Ti 1:6*

Where ev'rything is vanity, utter

Meaninglessness,*Ecc 1:2* without the Father God,

Hypocritical liars without sense,*1Ti 4:2*

Strange teachings without genuine object,*Heb 13:9*

Opposing Son for own satisfaction

With beguiling smooth talk and flattery.*Ro 16:18*

Religious officials opposed the Son

Because of the crowds that he attracted,

When no one would even listen to them,

Yet they could not say a word in reply,

The Son much too wise for them, looking fools,*Matt 22:46*

Even though their scholars had not taught him,*Jn 7:15*

His teaching still not his own but Father's,

As God at the burning bush taught Moses,*Exo 4:12*

And promised to teach his brother Aaron,*Exo 4:15*

Whom God gracious let speak for reluctant

Deliverer Moses' faltering lips,*Exo 6:30*

As God filled Bezalel with the Spirit,

And Oholiab, sure to teach others,*Exo 35:31*

To follow God's teaching that you may live,*Deut 4:1*

As retiring Samuel taught the people,*1Sam 12:23*

And Ezra came back from Babylon, well

Versed in God's law, to remind the people,*Ezra 7:6*

Humility making Son's teaching true,*Jn 7:16*

As he taught his hearers to teach, humbly,

Brothers, sisters, under one great Teacher,*Matt 23:8*

Son teaching only that learned from Father,

You, friends who know your master's business,*Jn 15:15*

No pretending ignorance any more,*Jn 15:22*

    Rejecting his words now clearly senseless,*Jn 15:24-25*

Like Jehoiakim burning in firepot

    Jeremiah's precious scrolls of Lord's word,*Jer 36:22*

Indeed, corrupt, decaying, death to follow,*Ro 5:12*

    Adam going his own way, ev'ryone

Following, until Son turns all around,*Ro 5:14*

    Bringing you life rather than your sure death,*Ro 5:15*

Teaching you love and God's holy order,

    Saving you from your own calamity.*Jn 5:14*

Revealing

The Son taught not rules but revealing truth,

    Living and active words that judge the heart,

Words that you cannot judge but that judge you,

    Revealing your own concealed condition,

In stories laden with hidden meaning,*Mk 4:2*

    Parable, analogy, metaphor,

Son explained only to his disciples,*Mk 4:33*

    Making his hearers reach for the good truth,

Inviting, not forcing, to different life,*1Th 4:7*

    Meeting your desire for goodness in acts,*2Th 1:11*

The Father knowing who are his in heart,*2Ti 2:19*

    Inviting a people to stand apart,*Ro 1:7*

Son appointing some to pursue his lost,*Ro 1:5*

    Remaining where you are, knowing the cost.*1Co 7:20*

The Teacher's stories accomplished purpose,

    Those desiring understood, others not,*Matt 13:11*

Heart coming first, those wanting getting more,

    The way learning always works, desire first,*Lk 8:18*

Parables allowing heartless to hear

    But not know, to see but not recognize,

As Isaiah foretold,*Isa 63:17* a hard-hearted

    People closing eyes and ears to the Son,*Lk 8:10*

Though sages and saints had yearned to hear him

    And see him without their chance to do so.*Matt 13:16*

The Father chose lowly and despised things,

    Even nonexistent, to nullify

Worldly things so that no one may boast,*1Co 1:28*

    Caring only for service to Father,*2Co 10:13*

Boasting only about others who know

    The Son,*2Co 10:14* the good work that others oft do,*2Co 10:15*

The Son's full willingness to die for you,*Gal 6:14*

    Knowing your weakness*2Co 11:30* and the Son's power.*2Co 12:9*

The Son explained how his parables worked,

    He as sower of seeds, his words the seeds,

Birds stealing seeds on hard paths, as hard hearts,*Matt 13:19*

    Heat killing seeds on thin soil, as troubled minds,*Matt 13:20*

Weeds choking seeds, as life and wealth worries,*Matt 13:22*

    But seeds on good soil huge crop, word pursued,*Matt 13:23*

Son fulfilling prophesy that he speak

    Hidden things,*Psa 78:2* desiring people unravel,*Matt 13:34*

As Moses on death said of Zebulun,

That they would feast on sand-hidden treasures,*Deut 33:19*

Or Obadiah hiding a hundred

Prophets in caves from murd'rous Jezebel,*1Kings 18:4*

That you would look for wisdom as hidden

Silver treasure, crying to know the Lord,*Proverbs 2:4*

Who gives you riches stored secret places,

That you may answer God's merciful call.*Isa 45:3*

Some learn constantly but ne'er accept truth,*2Ti 3:7*

Truth catching the worldly their craftiness,*1Co 3:19*

But the world's so-called wise thoughts are futile,*1Co 3:20*

So no putting up with exploiting fools;*2Co 11:19-20*

Stand for one another, discerning truth,

To do good, which is hard enough for you,*Heb 3:13*

And getting wisdom at all cost, though you

Have nothing else than its glorious crown.*Prov 4:7*

Healing

The Son's message spread quickly because his

Miraculous healing brought further crowds,*Matt 4:23*

Instant healing, horrible leprosy

Gone with a touch and word for the willing,

The Son come to set right for all who asked,*Mk 1:40*

Joyous, happy about the Son's coming,*Jn 16:21*

Confidence in rescue leading to joy,*1Pe 1:9*

Rejoicing in the good Father always,*Php 4:4*

Making others glad,*Ro 16:19* even for trials,*Matt 5:12*

Eager for others' confidence in truth,*3Jn 3*

Joyful espec'lly for rescued children, *2Jn 4*

Unbounded joy in one another's faith.*2Co 7:4*

The Son healed only those who wished healing,

Like Roman commander having servant

Healed on the Son's command from a distance,

His full faith amazing the willing Son,*Lk 7:1*

Begging royal official's son also

Healed from distance at moment the Son said,*Jn 4:46*

Son healing wherever he found the faith,

Asking invalid if he wished get well,

Then telling him to pick up mat and walk,*Jn 5:1*

Healing Peter's bedrid mother-in-law

With simple touch of hand, to rise and serve,*Matt 8:14*

Restoring paralyzed man on a mat,

The awed crowd right honoring the Father.*Matt 9:8*

Every illness, he cured instantly,

As Isaiah had foretold the Son would do,*Isa 53:4*

Taking infirmities, bearing disease,*Matt 8:16*

Healings just kept coming where faith revealed,*Matt 9:35*

Bleeding woman touching Son's cloak enough.*Lk 8:40*

The Son gave sight to two blind who's faith knew,*Matt 9:27*

Healed a man's shriveled hand,*Mk 3:1* another, too,*Lk 6:6*

Blind and mute man so he could talk and see,*Matt 12:22*

So none who tasted good news would turn back,*Heb 4:6*

Knowing its full power, great gift to keep,*Heb 6:4*

Holding to the Father's wonderful life,*Heb 3:12*

76

As God healed Abimelek's women to

    Bear children again, on Abra'm's prayer,*Gen 20:17*

For the Lord heals all your diseases,*Exo 15:26* as

    Moses' sister Miriam's leprosy,*Num 12:14*

As the Lord healed Marah's bitter waters,

    Showing Moses the cross wood to throw in,*Exo 15:25*

That God's freed people would in desert drink,

    The Lord's own holy life-giving water,

The Lord turned poor Naomi's bitter loss,*Ruth 1:20*

    To gleaning Ruth's rich husband Boaz gain,*Ruth 2:3*

The Lord healed old Jericho's poison spring

    When Elisha threw his salt into it,*2Kings 2:21*

And the Lord gave Hezekiah fifteen

    More years, sending Isaiah back to tell.*2Kings 20:5*

No Gilead balm, no physician there,

    Yet the Lord heals his people's mortal wounds.*Jer 8:22*

Son healed deaf and mute by putting fingers

    In ears, touching tongue, saying to open,*Mk 7:31*

Healed the blind by spitting and touching eyes,*Jn 9:1*

    Restored sight to two who asked forgiveness*Matt 20:29*

And to beggar who ran to Son in faith,*Mk 10:46*

    Healed Jerusalem's blind and disabled,*Matt 21:14*

Apostle Peter saying Son healed all,

    Having the Father's presence and power.*Acts 10:38*

Liberating

Humankind has long suffered deranged mind,

    Hallucination, odd seizure, possessed

Not of sound spirit and rationale but

    Tortured of mind and emotion, depressed,

Mentally disabled, unfit to act,

    As Nebuchadnezzar fell from king's rule

To eating grass for not acknowledging

    God most high as his authority's source,*Dan 4:32*

Not feigned craze like David before Achish,

    Marking doors and drooling down his beard

To escape the hostile king of Gath's wrath,*1Sam 21:13*

    And not such reasonable truth before fools,

To look insane, as Paul before Festus,*Acts 26:24*

    But genuine disability, craze.

The Son, though, healed these mental illnesses

    While casting out demonic influence,*Mk 1:32*

Restoring sanity for the faithful,*Mk 1:39*

    Often in spectacular fashion, so

Freeing a man of a demon who first

    Asked if the Son had come to destroy him,

Son ridding the man of silenced demon,

    Who came out with violent shake and shriek,*Lk 4:33*

Son casting demon legions out of two

    Men into pigs sent drowning into lake,*Matt 8:28*

And wild chained man living among the tombs,*Mk 5:1*

Demons begging Son not to torture them,_Mk 5:7_

Son also driving demon from mute man,

    Whose prompt talk amazed the bewildered crowd._Matt 9:32_

The Son gave his disciples author'ty

    To do same,_Lk 9:1_ seventy-two rejoicing

That even the enemy submitted,_Lk 10:17_

    Son replying to be etern'lly glad,_Lk 10:20_

So each rid of moral filth and evil,_Jas 1:21_

    Ignoring boast, pride, abuse, ingrat'tude,

Loveless, unforgiving, and slanderous,_2Ti 3:2_

    Letting the Son and Spirit clean them up,_1Co 6:9_

Corruption revealing perfect Father,_Ro 2:5_

    Thus to imitate good rather than evil._3Jn 11_

Son rid demons from a blind and mute man,_Matt 12:22_

    Beset daughter of a faithful woman,_Matt 15:21_

Boy demons oft cast into fire, water,_Lk 9:37_

    Son telling his incap'ble disciples

To ask Father's help to cast out demons,_Mk 9:28_

    'Specially in more-difficult cases._Lk 9:41_

When the Pharisees warned the Son to flee

    Persecution, he said he would press on,

Liberating many of their demons,

    For prophets must die in Jerusalem,_Lk 13:31_

That city of treacherous people, of

    Unprinc'pled prophets and profaning priests._Zeph 3:4_

Indeed, after the Son's resurrection,

    Apostles rid anyone of demons,_Acts 5:16_

Philip casting many shrieking demons,*Acts 8:5*

    Paul casting them from irksome female slave

Who earned her master money by predicting,*Acts 16:16*

    Father doing other wonders through Paul,

Cloth that touched Paul having the same power,*Acts 19:11*

    The good news healing mental illness, too.

Those not knowing good news, go wrong and die,*Ro 2:12*

    Their wrongs rightly angering the Father,*Col 3:6*

Who cannot justly excuse them from sin,*Heb 3:17-19*

    Warned no one gets away without the Son,*1Th 4:6*

Unjustified, unexcused wrongdoers,*Col 3:25*

    As you once were and knew it*Col 1:21* but are now

Following the Son's way, letting others

    Who ridicule you go their own hard way,*1Pe 4:5*

Wrongs obvious, although some sneaking up,*1Ti 5:24*

    Being slow to blame others for their wrongs,

But quick to share good news because friends are

    Better to deal with you than with the Son,*2Co 13:1*

Quietly showing your friends their missteps,*Matt 18:15*

    If continued, then others confront them,*Matt 18:16*

'Til no more quiet advice but reform;*Matt 18:17*

    All do wrong, some not seeing wrongs they do,*Jn 9:40*

All needing liberation, like Peter

    Walking free from Herod's guarded prison.*Acts 12:7*

Raising

The Son, though, did even even greater works than

　　To heal the sick and restore disabled,

Having such life within him, Father's own,

　　As to bring the fully dead back to life,

Reminding those who questioned his nature

　　That with his coming, blind could see, lame walk,

Diseased recover, deaf hear, dead to life,*Matt 11:4*

　　As raising widow's dead son from a bier

As it passed, heart moved, with his slightest touch,*Lk 7:11*

　　Astounding the people, thinking God there,

News spreading throughout the whole area,*Lk 7:16*

　　Bringing a dead boy back to life by touch,

As Elijah stretched himself three times on

　　The Zarephath widow's gone son for life,*1Kings 17:21*

Elisha prayed for Shunammite's dead child

　　Who sneezed seven times to come back to life,*2Kings 4:32*

And the Israelite dead man coming back

　　To life when thrown into Elisha's grave,

The man standing up when his body touched

　　The prophet's bones, as Spirit enabled,*2Kings 13:21*

Peter telling dead Tabitha get up,*Acts 9:40*

　　Eutychus from window fall, Paul to raise.*Acts 20:9*

Such wonders should build faith, but many still

　　Had none, just as the writings predicted,*Jn 12:37*

Even the disciples fearing drowning

Despite Jesus in the boat in the storm,*Matt 8:23*

At times having too little faith to heal,*Matt 17:14*

   When having little means losing what's left.*Matt 25:29*

But the Son still raised Jairius' daughter,

   When father showed he knew that the Son could;

While others laughed derisively at thought,

   Son took the girl's hand, and she came to life.*Lk 8:40*

The Son later heard friend Laz'rus was sick,

   But the Son tarried until Laz'rus died,

Waiting several more days to visit

   The family of his entombed dead friend;

Then, before crowd, Son called Laz'rus to life,

   Who asudden walked out wrapped in grave clothes,

Dead four days, stinking and stiff, now living,*Jn 11:1*

   Setting the 'mazed crowds on fire for God's Son.

Know this power of suddenly living

   Again after death, Son risen, alive,*Php 3:10*

Making your much pain and waiting worthwhile,

   Now reason to live, truly live as one should,*1Pe 1:3*

Son's coming back to life your sure rescue

   Because Son does the same wonder for you,*1Pe 3:21*

Either way, controlling ult'mate outcome,*Ro 14:7*

   Living forever coming through Son's choice,*1Co 15:21*

Son turning death on its head, death turning

   You back to Son, who always was your life.*1Co 15:22*

Attracting

The Son's good news and healing wonders brought

    Huge crowds, news spreading of him like wildfire,

All having something good to say of him,*Lk 4:14*

    Crowds pressing in so hard they could not eat,*Mk 3:20*

Wherever Son went, expecting he teach,*Mk 2:13*

    High on mountainside, large crowd gathering,*Matt 5:1*

Then following him down to see wonders.*Matt 8:1*

    So let your courage astonish others,*Acts 4:13*

Emboldened by Aaron's budding, blossomed,

    Almond-producing staff 'fore Israelites,*Num 17:8*

Prophetess Deborah's courage, sending

    Barak 'gainst Sisera, compelled to join,*Jdg 4:8*

Not letting deadly threats discourage you,*Acts 14:19*

    Teaching publicly*Acts 20:20* and teaching boldly,*Acts 28:30*

Reminding others of important points,*Ro 15:15*

    Authoritatively and resolute,*Tit 2:15*

Drawing the Son's powerful energy,*Col 1:28*

    Contending hard for all, known and unknown,*Col 2:1*

Courageously, not for show but results.*1Th 2:1*

    As the Son sought no attention, crowds came

Anyway to hear truth and see healing,*Lk 5:15*

    Whether at home, in Jerusalem, or

In wilderness,*Matt 4:25* no matter how far come,

    In great numbers,*Lk 6:17* witnessing Son's power,

Diseased straining to touch him for healing,*Mk 3:10*

Even digging a hole through low roof to

Let a paralyzed man down for healing,*Mk 2:3*

    The amazed people praising the Father.*Mk 2:12*

Word spread so wide the Son could not enter

    Town openly but must remain hidden,*Mk 1:45*

Trying to withdraw with his disciples,

    But crowds finding him, he pitying them,

Teaching and healing as they expected,*Lk 9:10*

    Though once, thousands trampled one another.*Lk 12:1*

Even when the Son crossed to wilderness,

    Large crowds followed for teaching and healing,*Matt 19:1*

Even up mountainsides, great crowds brought the sick,*Matt 15:29*

    The Son sometimes hiding to no avail,*Mk 7:24*

The more the Son keeping people quiet,

    The more news spread, crowds overwhelmed, amazed,*Mk 7:36*

His teaching delighting,*Mk 12:37* healing astounding,*Lk 13:17*

    His untameable message spreading far.

The Son, though, sought no popularity,*Lk 4:42*

    Hiding when he saw how large the crowds grew,

Still having compassion to heal their sick,*Matt 14:13*

    But hiding discretely on distant mount,

Not Elijah hiding from Jezebel

    In Mount Horeb cave, hearing God's whisper,*1Kings 19:8*

Not David hiding from murd'rous Saul in

    The strongholds at Horesh,*1Sam 23:19* praying to God,*Psa 54:1*

Not Gideon hiding from Midianites,

    Secretly threshing wheat in a winepress,*Jdg 6:11*

Nor convert Saul hiding from Damascan

    Jews, let down the night wall in a basket,*Acts 9:25*

But to avoid leading pop'lar revolt,*Jn 6:14*

    Often rising early to disappear,*Mk 1:35*

Preferring out-of-the-way getaways,*Lk 5:16*

    Sneaking away for quiet food and rest,*Mk 6:30*

Until the Son fled to the wilderness,*Jn 11:54*

    While people expected him to seek fame.*Jn 11:55*

People rightly sought the Son, relying

    On the creator of the universe,

Rather than senseless man-created things,*Ro 1:23*

    Rather than pursuing stomach or lust,*Php 3:19*

For food brings one no closer to Father,*1Co 8:8*

    Yet people chase dizzy after such things,

Thinking them alive, even ruled by them,*1Co 8:5*

    Devoting themselves to their strange worship,*Eph 5:7*

When you instead pursue the Son's good life,*Acts 17:16*

    Rejecting dead things for living Father,*1Th 1:9*

Running from ev'rything else,*1Co 10:14* Father first,*1Jn 5:20*

    Refusing to soil Father devotion,*2Co 6:16*

Not misleading the gullible into

    Pursuing others' dead and foolish things,*1Co 8:11*

Pointing others to Son, not lifeless things,*1Co 8:12*

    Restraining self to benefit others.*1Co 8:13*

Disciples

The Son drew disciples right away when

    Two following John, followed Son instead,*Jn 1:35*

The Son saying simply to come with him,*Jn 1:38*

    Andrew bringing his brother Simon to

See Messiah, who named Simon Peter,*Jn 1:40*

    Fishermen, now to fish for people 'stead,*Matt 4:18*

The Son astonishing them catching two

    Boatloads of fish, Peter seeing his sin,*Lk 5:8*

They prompt leaving their nets to follow Son,*Matt 4:20*

    Whose strange power frightened strong fishermen,*Lk 5:4*

As God called Moses from a burning bush,*Exo 3:4*

    Elijah threw his cloak on Elisha,

Who then slaughtered his twelve yoke of oxen,*1Kings 19:19*

    As you, too, should burn your old tools when called,

As servant Gehazi served Elisha,*2Kings 4:12*

    And Samuel ministered under Eli,*1Samuel 3:1*

Boy thrice hearing the Lord's call, swift

    To answer here am I, here am I, here,*1Samuel 3:4*

As Isaiah answered when the Lord sought

    Prophet to send warning to his people.*Isa 6:8*

Discipleship comes at cost but with wage,*Mk 6:8*

    Others supporting your good-news teaching,*Matt 10:11*

So accept what those whom you teach offer,*Lk 10:8*

    Sharing word free if must, but moving on,*Mk 6:10*

No regret,*Lk 9:4* teaching deserving fair wage,*1Ti 5:17*

Sharing duly in teaching's benefit,*1Co 9:10*

Mater'al reward for spir'tual teaching,*1Co 9:11*

Although fine, too, if you instead decline,*1Co 9:14*

Teaching free, earning a special reward,*1Co 9:17*

Though others pay when teachers teach for free.*2Co 11:8*

The Son quickly recruited James and John

Out of a boat with their father and men,*Matt 4:21*

Philip, who brought his brother Nathanael,

Who recognized the Son as the King come.*Jn 1:43*

Levi, Matthew, out tax collector's booth,

Son dining at Matthew's house with sinners,*Matt 9:9*

Drawing these disciples up mountainside

To appoint famous but oft-clueless twelve,*Mk 3:13*

To tell of him that many may rely,*Lk 10:2*

Giving them his power others to heal.*Mk 3:16*

All, Son, too, serve not self but the Father,*Jn 6:38*

Doing as Father says for his honor,*Matt 7:21*

Son noticing those who do for Father,*Matt 7:23*

What you do in proving your Father wise,*Matt 11:19*

Doing, not listening, counting as good,*Jas 1:23*

Father favoring those doing what said,*Jas 1:25*

Love shown by acting, not simply talking,*1Jn 3:17*

An example for others in doing.*1Ti 4:11*

When things got hard and many left the Son,

He asked if the twelve would leave, too, Peter

Replying they had no one to whom go,*Jn 6:67*

Though 'fraid of dying by stone with the Son,*Jn 11:15*

Yet out they went boldly telling many

> Good news while healing many diseases,*Mk 6:7*

As Son directed to share the kingdom,*Lk 9:2*

> Sending many more of his disciples,*Lk 10:1*

Even saying to bring the dead to life,*Matt 10:8*

> Until at the last supper, the Son washed

His disciples' feet in modeled service,*Jn 13:2*

> Peter's confused protest notwithstanding.*Jn 13:8*

Father's Spirit is your servant power,*Lk 24:49*

> To tell others good news, as best you do,*Acts 1:8*

That power beating enemy's power,*Lk 10:19*

> Keeping you alive and uncorrupted,*2Co 13:4*

Your weakness perfecting Father's power,*2Co 12:8*

> You weak so that you have the Son's power,*2Co 12:9*

The Spirit not leaving you timid,*2Ti 1:7* but

> Overflowing with the Spirit's power,*Ro 15:13*

Crediting Spirit power for good done,*Ro 15:18*

> Asking Father for power to endure.*Col 1:10*

Feeding

As God gave Moses heaven's manna,*Exo 16:14* taste

> Of coriander seed and honey,*Exo 16:31* in

Flakes gathered each morning save Sabbath,*Exo 16:25*

> To sustain through desert wandering,

David and his men ate Ahimelek's

> Consecrated bread when in Saul's flight,*1Samuel 21:4*

God had ravens feed Elijah when he

    Hid from Ahab in the Kerith Ravine,*1Kings 17:4*

Elisha fed one hundred men from few

    Loaves set before them, with more left over,*2Kings 4:42*

So the Son also fed amazed people,

    Calling their attention to the good news,

Satisfying their mater'al hunger

    While more significantly feeding souls,

The disciples saying send hungry crowds

    Away from remote place to buy their food,*Matt 14:15*

But the Son replying to give the crowd

    Something to eat, testing their faith in him,*Mk 6:37*

Turning to Philip, if understood,*Jn 6:5*

    Wanting disciples to rely on him,*Jas 2:14*

Actions testing, proving your faith in him,*Jas 2:18*

    Faith dying without supporting action,*Jas 2:26*

Reward following, not preceding, faith,*Jas 2:20*

    Showing who full embraces the good news,*Jas 3:13*

Helping the hungry poor,*Gal 2:10* orphans, widows,*Jas 1:27*

    Caring for your family,*1Ti 5:4* your household,*1Ti 5:8*

Proving useful so that you help others,*Eph 4:28*

    Your confidence overflowing to help,*Acts 6:1-6*

Risking your own life when necessary*Php 2:30*

    To supply what others fail to supply,*1Co 16:17*

So that your light rises in darkness and

    Your midnight becomes like the noonday sun,*Isa 58:10*

Your people repair the broken walls and

Restore streets so that they 'gain have dwellings,*Isa 58:12*

Serving ev'ryone to win to the Son,*1Co 9:19*

Your work impressing, pointing to Father.*Col 3:22*

The disciples replied that buying bread

Cost half year's wages, missing Son's power,*Jn 6:7*

Though finding five loaves of bread and two fish,*Lk 9:13*

Andrew wondering how far it would go,*Jn 6:8*

But Son took loaves and fish, thanked Father, and

Broke the loaves, feeding five thousand men plus

Women and children, twelve baskets left o'er,*Matt 14:17*

Foreshadowing Son's body feeding all,

As bread continually remained on

The tabernacle's blue-cloth-spread table,*Num 4:7*

And Joseph fed through seven years' famine

From Pharaoh's overflowing storehouses,*Gen 41:54*

And Elisha filled all the widow's jars

From a single small jar of olive oil,*2Kings 4:4*

And fed the company of prophets in

Famine, putting flour in a poisoned pot.*2Kings 4:38*

So stop worrying, lest forget good news,*Matt 13:22*

Not about what you eat, drink, or e'en wear,*Lk 12:22*

For birds eat without worry, won't then you?*Matt 6:26*

Father cares for flowers, better care you,*Matt 6:28*

Worry not adding single hour to life,*Lk 12:25*

The Father supplying your ev'ry need,*Matt 6:31*

When do as he directs*Matt 6:33* without fear for

Tomorrow, worrying about itself,*Matt 6:34*

90

Each day at a time,$_{Matt\ 6:34}$ forget anxiety,

 Knowing that you are living forever.$_{Lk\ 21:34}$

The Son later drew crowd up mountainside

 For days without food, 'gain growing hungry,$_{Matt\ 15:29}$

Son asking disciples for seven loaves

 And few small fish that they had among them,$_{Mk\ 7:1}$

Once again thanking Father, breaking loaves,

 Feeding thousands with baskets left over,$_{Matt\ 15:36}$

Son's great power hard disciple lesson,

 Why Son repeated his thousands feeding.$_{Matt\ 16:9}$

Cause none to stumble, whether foe or friend,$_{1Co\ 10:32}$

 Putting no obstacle in 'nother's way,$_{Ro\ 14:13}$

Nor forcing others over traditions,$_{Ro\ 14:14}$

 Nor distressing others o'er what you do;$_{Ro\ 14:15}$

Do as you wish, between you and Father,

 Not upsetting those who think you should not.$_{Ro\ 14:22}$

Prayer

Just as Abraham's senior servant prayed

 That God would grant Isaac a good wife,$_{Gen\ 24:12}$

Isaac prayed that Rebekah would conceive,$_{Gen\ 25:21}$

 Jacob prayed that Esau would forgive him,$_{Gen\ 32:9}$

Moses prayed that the Lord would remove fire$_{Num\ 11:2}$

 And snakes,$_{Num\ 21:7}$ and not destroy brother Aaron,$_{Deut\ 9:20}$

Joram and Jehoshaphat sought 'Lisha

 Pray for vict'ry, and God sent blood rivers,$_{2Kings\ 3:23}$

Jonah prayed from inside fish belly,*Jonah 2:1* from

    Deep distress in the realm of the dead,*Jonah 2:2*

The Son spoke constantly with his Father

    While also teaching others how to pray,

Rising early to talk with his Father,*Mk 1:35*

    Withdrawing to pray,*Lk 5:16* admonishing prayer

As lone answer for enduring troubles,*Mk 9:28*

    Ev'rything done through and for the Father,

Thanking Father for restoring Laz'rus

    So those present would know Father's doing,*Jn 11:41*

Telling his disciples that he asked the

    Father to save them from the enemy,*Lk 22:31*

Driving dishonest merchants from Temple

    Courtyard to keep prayer house over market,*Jn 2:13*

Overturning money changers' tables

    To keep house for prayer, not den of robbers.*Matt 21:12*

As Samson prayed for one last strength, revenge

    On his Philistines captors to exact,*Jdg 16:28*

Hannah prayed to conceive her child Samuel,*1Sam 2:1*

    Temple priest Eli thinking Hannah drunk,*1Sam 1:13*

David prayed turn Ahithophel's counsel

    Foolish for his rebel son Absalom,*2Sam 15:31*

So ask on all occasions for all things,

    Especially for those who rely on Son,*Eph 6:18*

Thankfully,*Php 4:6* to know Father's will for you,*Col 1:9*

    Persistently,*Col 4:2* night and day, for your faith,*1Th 3:10*

As Elijah seven times sent servant

Back to see coming rain for which he prayed,*1Kings 18:44*

As Jehoash at Elijah's command

Struck arrows three, better six, times on ground,*2Kings 13:18*

Pray continually,*1Th 5:17* you for others,*1Th 5:25*

That Father enable his will to do,*2Th 1:11*

For help,*1Ti 5:5* for others,*2Ti 1:3* rejoining others,*Ro 1:9*

Trusting that you will receive what you asked,*Matt 21:22*

While right with the Father to get answers,*Jas 5:16*

Asking what the Father wants you to do,*1Jn 5:14*

Not numbering troops when God forbids, as

Joab warned David,*1Chron 21:3* God three options give,*1Chron 21:10*

And David built altar on Araunah's

Threshing floor, avenging angel appeased,*1Chron 21:20*

Asking with others who rely on Son,*Matt 18:19*

Secretly,*Matt 6:6* in brief,*Matt 6:7* Father knowing needs,*Matt 6:8*

For all, including the authorities,*1Ti 2:1*

For your own healing*Jas 5:13* and others' healing,*Jas 5:16*

For good mental health*3Jn 2* and to love others,*1Th 3:12*

Wrestling with asking,*Col 4:12* inviting God's rule,*Lk 11:1*

Audaciously,*Lk 11:5* expecting your receipt,*Lk 11:9*

Relentlessly,*Lk 18:1* for justice,*Lk 18:7* Son honor,*2Th 1:12*

In rev'rent submission,*Heb 5:7* to know Son's love,*Eph 3:17*

That the good news spread,*2Th 3:1* all rely on Son.*Ro 10:1*

As Hezekiah prayed, face to the wall,

Not to die at Isaiah's prophesy,*2Kings 20:2*

Nehemiah prayed for returned exiles,*Neh 1:4*

After Israel had sinned against the Lord,*2Kings 17:7*

Who sent them to exile apart from him,*2Kings 17:23*

And Job prayed for God to forgive his friends,*Job 42:10*

The Son also prayed with the Father,

To honor Father as Father did Son,*Jn 17:1*

How Father allowed Son grant life fore'er,*Jn 17:2*

Which is to know the Father and the Son,*Jn 17:3*

Finishing Son's work honoring Father,

So Father honored Son as world began,*Jn 17:4*

Honoring Father, Son had shown Father

To those Father gave him who obeyed them.*Jn 17:6*

This unity Son sought, that whoever

Welcomes a child like the Son, welcomes Son,*Matt 18:5*

So welcome another without complaint,*1Pe 4:9*

Speak freely,*2Co 6:11* withholding no kindnesses;*2Co 6:12*

Open wide your heart,*2Co 6:13* making others room,*2Co 7:2*

Ready to live and die with another,*2Co 7:3*

Taking pride in others,*2Co 7:4* sharing your joy,*2Co 7:7*

Being just as others wish you to be,

While finding them as you want them to be,*2Co 12:20*

Refreshing one another,*Phm 20* more than asked,*Phm 21*

Desiring their benefit, like parent,*2Co 12:14*

Not burdening others,*2Co 12:16* exploiting them,*2Co 12:17*

But every favor voluntary,*Phm 14*

With deep love and compassion for others,*2Co 2:4*

Submitting to others, revering Son,*Eph 5:21*

Remembering others,*Php 1:3* glad for the Son,*Php 1:7*

Thinking well how others rely on Son,*Col 2:5*

Your joy and crown,*1Th 2:19* walking in their footsteps,*2Co 12:18*

Not defending but strengthening,*2Co 12:19* sharing,*Col 4:7*

Remembering your good times together,*1Th 3:6*

Longing to see one another again,*1Th 2:17*

Encouraging one another daily,*Heb 3:13*

Building up the disheartened,*1Th 5:11* showing love,*Phm 7*

Patiently and carefully,*2Ti 4:2* making strong.*Ro 1:11*

Son prayed Father care for his disciples,*Jn 17:9-10*

Asking Father protect and unite them,*Jn 17:11*

Honoring Father for protecting them,*Jn 17:12*

Speaking to Father for all followers,*Jn 17:20*

Praying Father keep all given him, to

See Father honor Son loved before world,*Jn 17:24*

To make Father apparent to all, so

All would love Father as Father loves Son.*Jn 17:25*

Book 6: Character

Sacred

The Son's mission revealed his character,

    When knowing who the Son is may mean more

Than knowing what the Son has done and does,

    Sacred, hallowed, different, set apart,

Numinous, supernat'ral, outside of

    And above all things, inspiring wonder,

Amazement, astonishment, reverence,

    With Father before time and place began,

Is Father in way beyond understand,*Jn 1:1*

    Existing before patriarch Abr'am,

As the One incorporeal I Am,

    YHWH, tetragrammaton, no need to

Justify, rationalize, or explain,

    Without whom none other would ever be,*Jn 8:58*

Over ev'rything, forever honored,*Ro 9:5*

    Ultimate power and authority,*Col 2:10*

Like the holy ground on which Moses stood,

    No closer, sandals off, 'fore burning bush,*Exo 3:5*

The sacred garments high priest Aaron wore,*Exo 28:2*

    Breastpiece, ephod, robe, tunic, turban, sash,*Exo 28:4*

The sacred anointing oil, perfumer

    Blend of fine spices and olive oil,*Exo 30:22*

The holy place Joshua fell facedown

    Before the Lord's own army commander.*Joshua 5:14*

The Son's sacred nature demands that we

    Act right for his good Father who sees all,*Matt 6:1*

Pure and patient, loving, sincere, and kind,*2Co 6:6*

    Doing right when people think doing wrong,*2Co 13:7*

Nazirite vow not outwardly, abstain

    From fermented drink,*Num 6:3* but inwardly pure,

Being poor but while making others rich,

    Having nothing but possessing his all,*2Co 6:8*

Practicing purity,*2Co 7:1* God's word helping,*2Ti 3:16*

    Like Nehemiah examining and

Repairing Jerusalem's broken walls,*Neh 2:13*

    Guarded sword and spear, fam'ly by fam'ly,*Neh 4:13*

So the Spirit guards you, as you clean up,*Ro 15:16*

    While revealing for you Father and Son,

Only seeing the Father if you try,*Heb 12:14*

    Father and Son one, same sacred substance,*Jn 10:30*

Seeing the Father's Son, seeing Father,*Jn 12:45*

    Knowing the Father's Son, knowing Father,*Jn 14:7*

Son in Father, Father Son, one essence,*Jn 14:10*

    Ev'rything the Father's also the Son's,*Jn 16:15*

Son invis'ble Father's perfect image,

Over all as Father is over all,*Col 1:15*

Radiating Father's exact honor,

    Sustaining all bound for destruction 'til

Son intervened to save all for Father,*Heb 1:3*

    Sacred Father's fullness in bod'ly form.*Col 2:9*

Father invites you to belong to Son,*Ro 1:6*

    With your destiny to be like the Son's,*Ro 8:29*

Your concerns those of God, rather than those

    Stumbling blocks, fearful Peter borne, of men,*Matt 16:23*

Chosen in the Son according to plan,*Eph 1:11*

    From your conception's moment, sharing Son,*Gal 1:15*

Listening to the Son with Spirit's help,*1Pe 1:2*

    Following Father's plan without stumble,

Son's rich welcome to your prepared place,

    Where you will live joyously forever.*2Pe 1:10*

The Son will not change, same then as today,

    Same on into the future, forever,*Heb 13:8*

The Father making so from before time,

    Son not slowly earning his qualities

But full character present from day one,*Jude 24*

    All having same spiritual food and drink

From the rock, the Son who was right with them,*1Co 10:3*

    Moses striking the rock to bring water,*Num 20:11*

Once, on God's command, not in anger, twice,

    Lest, like Moses, not enter promised land,*Num 20:12*

The same rock crushing man's corrupt kingdoms,*Dan 2:34*

    Like Micaiah condemned bad king Ahab,

About whom prophet never had good to say,*1Kings 22:18*

    Not cleverly devised story but seen,

Heard, touched, in his astonishing power,*2Pe 1:16*

    Once only through prophets, but today here,*Heb 1:2*

All garbage compared to knowing the Son,*Php 3:8*

    All that anyone or thing could e'er be,*1Jn 5:20*

Not sole human, that God should lie, and not

    Sole human, that once made should change his mind.*Num 23:19*

Rules are not your father god;*Ro 2:20* the Father

    Chose you before you kept or broke the rules,*Ro 9:10*

Your rescue depending on his mercy,

    Not on what you do or how you do it;*Ro 9:16*

Keeping rules has no return, did not work,*Gal 2:18*

    Spirit not rule keeping but gift unearned,*Gal 3:2*

Not do this, do that, rule for this, rule that,

    Here a little, there a little, ensnared,*Isa 28:13*

No perfect keepers but perfect Father,*Matt 5:20*

    Perfect Son, perfect Spirit, perfect gift.*Jn 5:9*

You have set out from darkest Mount Sinai,*Num 10:12*

    To walk free into the Son's perfect light.

Human

While Son is sacred, he is also man,

    Tangible, corporeal, flesh in form,

Like the Lord God walking among the trees in

    Cool of paradise's Eden Garden,*Gen 3:8*

Father's living Word in body substance,*Jn 1:14*

    Father known through Son,*Jn 1:18* Isaiah foretold,*Mk 1:1*

Yet descended from David, also told,*Ro 1:3*

    Revealing the Father to those like you,*Matt 11:27*

Not dwelling only specially among

    Chosen Israelite people out Egypt,*Exo 29:45*

No longer need for special meeting place,*Heb 9:1*

    Curtained off from all, symbol of promise,*Heb 9:3*

Only priests enter, borne of animal blood,*Heb 9:7*

    Temple foreshadowing what was to come,*Heb 9:8*

Gifts and blood temp'rary 'til new order,*Heb 9:10*

    To direct encounter Father and Son,*Heb 13:10*

Like Jacob struggling night with God and man,

    Only Israel named for having overcome,*Gen 32:28*

Solomon at Temple dedication

    Ask God really dwell on earth with humans?*2Chron 6:18*

Nebuchadnezzar's astrologers knew

    Gods do not live with men, to reveal truth,*Dan 2:11*

'Cept God of all who made his promise to

    Walk among you, Immanuel, your God,*Lev 26:12*

Subject to ev'ry human temptation,

    Empathizing but never succumbing,*Heb 4:15*

The Lord your God with you first in battle,

    Your King's own shout, his war cry, among you,*Num 23:21*

Great, fearsome, awesome, hard to encounter,

    Requiring you keep your camp holy,

Free of indecency, lest turn from you,*Deut 23:14*

Yet among you, not terror,_{Deut 7:21} but as man, and

As man, Son showing how a child relates

To loving Father, receiving Father,_{Jn 3:35}

Giving the Father reason to love more,

Giving the Father all, indeed one's life,_{Jn 10:17}

As the Israelites gave wholeheartedly

To build God's Temple, so David rejoiced,_{1Chron 29:9}

And when the priests brought up the ark, the Lord's

Glory filled Temple so priests could not serve,_{2Chron 5:14}

Son come from the Father, returning_{Jn 16:28}

To a Father who too good for the world,_{Jn 17:25}

Returning all Father gave to the Son,_{Jn 17:10}

Father committing his all to the Son,_{Lk 10:22}

Son knowing and obeying his Father,_{Jn 8:55}

As Son told Jerusalem officials

Who tried to stone him that he was Father's,_{Jn 10:36}

As you are Father's spiritual children,_{Jn 1:12}

Not servant Hagar-born children of flesh,

Like wild-donkey Ishmael, against all, all

Against him, living hostile toward brothers,_{Gen 16:1}

Instead peaceful children of God's promise,_{Rom 9:8}

Following the Father's Spirit as child,_{Ro 8:14}

Spirit squelching fear of Father's anger,_{Ro 8:15}

You and creation groaning as you wait

Eagerly for the Father's adoption._{Ro 8:22}

Father does no better than make you child,_{1Jn 3:1}

Surprising many children he chooses,_{Ro 9:24}

Ancestry ignored, Father's promise only,*Ro 9:7*

    Ev'rything child inherits—ev'rything,*Gal 4:30*

Especially, best gift, Father's Spirit,*Gal 4:6*

    Father giving his children himself, all.*Rev 21:6*

Father chose his Son, as Father chose you,*Heb 1:5*

    Pledging Son's appointment, perfect fore'er,*Heb 7:28*

As Father's first born in the world, angel

    Worshipped,*Heb 1:6* above e'en angelic being,*Heb 1:4*

Son, not angels, sitting beside Father,*Heb 1:13*

    The Son's just rule to proceed forever,*Heb 1:8*

Son made human to begin world anew,

    Starting world over again without death,*Col 1:18*

The Son without earthly genealogy,

    With neither beginning nor end of life.*Heb 7:1*

Father loves you, keeping his Son for you,

    Showering you with glor'ous peace and love,*Jude 1*

Hiding his treasures in the Son for you,*Col 2:3*

    Making the Son your head, directing you,*Col 2:19*

Your life in Son,*2Ti 1:1* remembered, back to life,*2Ti 2:8*

    Old and worn disappearing, all things new,*2Co 5:17*

Brought back to Son whom you share with others,*2Co 5:18*

    Given good news of your new beginnings,*2Co 5:19*

Son protecting you from evil if turned,*1Jn 5:18*

    Joining Father freely, confidently,*Eph 3:12*

Speaking Son's message of right with Father,*2Co 5:20*

    in Son, showing the Father's perfection.*2Co 5:21*

Liberator

Yet Son came not just to reveal Father,

But to rescue you, liberate the world,

The Father so loving you and his world

To give his only Son for you to trust,

None to die but instead live forever,

Freed from the world's greatest enemy death,*Jn 3:16*

As sole way for all to return to him,*Col 1:20*

As Son told a Samaritan woman

Drawing uselessly from old Jacob's well,

Jesus is the Christ, Messiah to come,*Jn 4:25*

Whose living water ever wells to life

Eternal, to worship in Spirit and truth,*Jn 4:24*

Everlasting Lord, our God, Holy One,

Who will never die but live eternal,*Hab 1:12*

Emancipator bringing freedom news,*Mk 1:1*

Savior whom Magi East sought, to bow down,*Matt 2:1*

Long known to come in tiny Bethlehem,*Matt 2:4*

From David's royal line, your only chance,*Matt 1:1*

As Nebuchadnezzar saw God's Son save

Shadrach, Meshach, and Abednego,*Dan 3:25* from

Furnace so hot that it killed the soldiers

Who threw in the Son's rescued prisoners,*Dan 3:22*

And as the Lord moved Cyrus, Persia's king,

To send Israel back to the promised land.*Ezra 1:1*

Watch out! When others see you Son made free,

Enslave you again with old ways, they will,*Gal 2:4*

So give no quarter, no stronghold to them,*Gal 2:5*

Not their rules not to handle, taste, or touch,*Col 2:21*

Nor judge you condemned by your eat or drink,*Col 2:16*

Whether one day more than another day,*Ro 14:5*

Whether meat or abstain,*Ro 14:6* when earth is yours,

Ev'rything your rich gift from the Father.*1Co 10:25*

Prophets had long sought the people's Savior,

Spirit foretelling through them how he comes,*1Pe 1:10*

Yet when the Savior came, some thought him John,

Others resurrected prophet 'Lijah,

Disciple Peter, though, Messiah, Christ;*Mk 7:27*

Pharisees, David's son, but Jesus that

David called the Savior his own Master,*Matt 22:41*

Even high priest Caiaphas charging him

Messiah, God's Son, under living oath,*Matt 26:63*

Unwitting recognition, prophesy,

Apostle Peter confirming Son One,

Able alone to save from certain death,*Acts 4:12*

As Moses sang to Israelite 'ssembly,

Before up Mount Nebo he climbed to die,

Not like Jeshurun to grow sassy fat,

One's Father, rock and Savior, to reject,*Deut 32:15*

But cry out from Pharaoh's oppression,*Exo 1:11*

Bricks without straw,*Exo 5:8* no day of worship rest,

All male children under a death edict,

Needing midwives from genocide protect,*Exo 1:17*

Drawn like infant Moses from the waters,*Exo 2:5*

    God sending our deliv'rer and Savior,*Isaiah 19:20*

He, the One Lord, apart from whom you have

    No other hope, no other Redeemer,*Isaiah 43:11*

Proclamation made to earth's ends, Zion,

    Your Savior comes, your reward, him.*Isaiah 62:11*

Master

The Son came without sentiment, advice,

    But as Master, ruler, beyond ignore,*Jn 13:13*

Not mean dictator but author'ty's peace,*Heb 7:1*

    Higher any other, utter Master,*Php 2:9*

His triumphal Jerusalem entry,

    Your King coming righteous, victorious,

But lowly, riding colt foal of donkey,*Zech 9:9*

    Signifying rule, confirmation shouts,

Stirring all Jerusalem, Savior come,

    As so long awaited, so long foretold,*Mk 11:1*

Pharisees demanding quiet crowd,

    But Son saying stones would then 'stead cry out.*Lk 19:39*

Pontius Pilate knew Son a king, said so,*Jn 18:37*

    Greater than Temple, Master of Sabbath,*Lk 6:1*

So obv'ous rule all, least to greatest, know,*Heb 8:11*

    Sway o'er each one of you, no way your own,*2Co 5:10*

Ruling that which you do not even see,*Heb 2:5*

    Patient, but not to make him wait for you,*2Pe 3:9*

Returning soon to decide whither each goes,_{Php 4:5}

    Master even death, greatest victory,_{1Co 15:26}

When done, putting himself under Father,

    Father ev'rything,_{1Co 15:28} together in Son,_{Eph 1:8}

Crediting you for all things Son did right,_{Ro 4:6}

    Law and prophets point Father's perfect way,_{Ro 2:21}

As when Hilkiah found book of the law

    In the Temple during Josiah reign,_{2Kings 22:8}

Who wept and tore his robes o'er transgressions,_{2Kings 22:11}

    And seeing, God averted disaster,_{2Kings 22:19}

Though man instead desire a human king,

    Rejecting their all-powerful Lord God,_{1Sam 10:19}

When better that king, like Hezekiah,

    Acknowledge alone God over all,_{2Kings 19:15}

Like Judah's Jehoshaphat, stand 'ssembly

    To pronounce Lord God as ruler of all,_{2Chron 20:6}

Lot in Sodom bowing before angels,_{Gen 19:1}

    Jacob bowing seven times 'fore Esau,_{Gen 33:3}

Governor Joseph's brothers face to ground,_{Gen 43:26}

    Fleeing Israelites bowing in worship,_{Exo 4:31}

Ruth face to ground 'fore ben'factor Boaz,_{Ruth 2:10}

    E'en David prostrate to en'my king Saul._{1Sam 28:14}

Celebrant

The Son is also priest, minister, great

    Celebrant over his Father's house,_{Heb 10:21}

Not claiming, Father granting him that role,

That Son point you to Father forever,*Heb 5:5*

Son God's first, chief, and greatest celebrant,*Heb 5:10*

Indestructible, unsurpassable,

Infinitely greater line than those

Before, all law teachers, rule keepers all,*Heb 7:1*

The Son to emulate, closer to God,

God incarnate, chief priest forever, all,*Heb 6:19*

As Melchizedek was God's priest most high,*Gen 14:18*

Like high priests of old, anointed, ordained,*Lev 21:10*

Hilkiah high priest finding Temple's law,*2Kings 22:8*

Eliashib high priest rebuild Sheep Gate,*Neh 3:1*

Jozadak's son Joshua high priest,

Standing 'fore Lord's angel, Satan aside.*Zech 3:1*

With Son priest, fight the good fight to the end,*2Ti 4:6*

Your obedience making all happy,*Ro 16:19*

Running the race not to waste but for prize,*1Co 9:24*

For crown not temp'rary but lasts forever,*1Co 9:25*

Not aimlessly like boxer beating air,*1Co 9:26*

But focused to win your authentic prize,*1Co 9:27*

Standing test,*2Co 2:9* right ev'rything, ev'rywhere,*Col 1:10*

Striving to do good for everyone,*1Th 5:15*

Working hard not to burden anyone,*2Th 3:7*

Busy rather than idle, earning keep,*2Th 3:11*

Diligent to end,*Heb 6:11* tireless, not lazy,*Heb 6:12*

Done one, doing next, doing your duty,*Lk 17:7*

For sleep, slumber, fold your hands to rest, and

Poverty comes quickly like an armed man.*Prov 24:33*

The Son will forever remain God's priest,*Heb 7:20*

Permanent honor and celebration,*Heb 7:23*

Partic'pant leader, one to emulate,

Intervening with the Father for you,*Heb 7:25*

His presence as good as anything gets,*Heb 7:26*

Paid all without debt, all to celebrate,*Heb 7:27*

Sitting 'side Father, you to represent,*Heb 8:2*

His Father worship, giving all he had.*Heb 8:3*

Thank Father you are free of old desire,*Ro 6:18*

Consigned then to die, now live forever,*Ro 5:21*

Celebrating him, even as you fight,*Heb 12:4*

Trusting that his good beats your former bad,*Ro 12:21*

Worshipping Father as Son honored him,

Giving ev'rything for him, like priest Son.

Guide

As Son leads you, celebrating good news,

Son also guides you, dying that you live,*Jn 10:10*

While telling you why, calling you to him,

Not as stranger but as your dearest friend,*Jn 10:3*

Trusted advisor, knowing who listens,

Not paid but paying to serve you, committed,*Jn 10:12*

Open door through which to run to safe place,

Safe even from death for all who enter,*Jn 10:7*

Guiding as Lord guided wand'ring Israel

By pillar of day cloud and fire night,*Exo 13:21*

Hobab as Moses' desert eyes and guide,*Num 10:31*

Uzzah and Ahio guided ark cart,*1Chron 13:7*

The Lord showing the blind unknown new paths,

Turning rough paths smooth, dark ways into light,*Isa 42:16*

Neither hunger, thirst, desert sun nor heat,*Isa 49:10*

But soothing spring whose waters never fail,*Isa 58:11*

As Moses at God's invitation struck

Christ rock out of which endless water flow.*Exo 17:6*

As the Son guides and counsels you, so, too,

The Father disciplines those whom he loves,*Heb 12:6*

So endure hardship as your discipline,*Heb 12:7*

Proving you Father's legitimate child;*Heb 12:8*

Submit more to spiritual discipline,*Heb 12:9*

Father disciplining only for good,*Heb 12:10*

Unpleasant, but when accepted, for good,*Heb 12:11*

Strengthening weak spiritual character,*Heb 12:12*

The Spirit supplying self-discipline,*2Ti 1:7*

Avoiding arrogance,*1Co 4:21* able to lead

Others to discipline,*Tit 1:8* seeking counsel,*1Co 11:32*

For nations fall for lack of sound counsel,

While many advisors make for wise choice,*Prov 11:14*

Listening to the Father's words for heart,*Heb 12:5*

Knowing from discipline that Son loves you,

As he disciplines only those he loves.*Rev 3:19*

Reject counsel from frauds and thieves having

Their own agenda to steal, kill, destroy,*Jn 10:8*

Blind guides, misleading you, rough paths, astray,*Isa 9:16*

    Like Saul consulting medium guidance,*1Chron 10:13*

Endor woman ghost Samuel rising, 'gainst

    Own order, conjuring dead to lead dead,*1Sam 28:9*

When you should instead, like good Josiah,

    Rid mediums and spiritists, Lord led.*2Kings 23:24*

Don't fret if Son welcomes unlike others,

    'Cause listening to him, they are like you;*Jn 10:16*

You'll know when the Son speaks to you if you

    Desire to do so, desire paradise.*Jn 10:27*

The Son guides, so listen;*Heb 13:20* stop stumbling around,

    Because the Son has solved all your problems.*Matt 9:36*

No looking because it gets you trouble;*Matt 5:27*

    Turn away, or you're lost before you know.*Matt 5:29*

No walking down that road, or you are done;*Matt 18:8*

    Dabble with wrongdoing, and you're enslaved.*Mk 9:43*

Don't indulge now, lose paradise later;*Mk 9:47*

    Leave all your wrongdoing now while you can.*Jn 8:11*

Rather than hard on others, watch yourself;*Gal 6:1*

    Your enemy tempts, courting your own death.*Jas 1:13*

You're not so strong, so you better watch out;*1Co 10:12*

    The Father always gives you a way out.*1Co 10:13*

Avoid sexual immorality;*Heb 12:17*

    Your body is the Father's, not cheating.*1Co 6:13*

Chasing riches will lead you to ruin;*1Ti 6:9*

    Loving money draw you from the Father,*1Ti 6:10*

As Hezekiah showed envoys all his

Many storehouse treasures, all then his loss.*Isa 39:6*

The Son searches not for big crowds but for you,

Leaving ninety nine for one wand'ring off,*Matt 18:12*

Just as the Father wants not to lose one,*Matt 18:14*

Celebrating more when one follows Son,*Lk 15:7*

As all ran at Son's death, as predicted,

But then all returned when the Son came back,*Matt 26:31*

So you should eager return to your guide

For reward greater than you imagine,*1Pe 5:4*

If you but listen to your guide the Son,*Matt 25:32*

Who holds the kingdom's door open for you,*Rev 3:20*

Against soul, your mind, will, and emotions,

That your spirit, from God's Spirit, 'stead rule,*Ro 5:5*

Spirit in you, pursuing his desires,

So Spirit bring you back to life like Son,*Ro 8:11*

Spirit speaking when you rely on Son,*Eph 1:13*

Guiding you,*1Th 4:8* showing what Father prepares

For those who love him,*1Co 2:9* knowing God's secrets,*1Co 2:10*

Knowing God's thoughts like your spirit knows yours.*1Co 2:11*

So do not offend the Father's Spirit;*Eph 4:30*

You share the Spirit's new promise of life.*2Co 3:6*

Transfigured

The Son has countless profound attributes,

Infinitely more than one count or know,

Lighting the whole world and its ev'ry life,*Jn 8:12*

Revealed to disciples Peter, James, John,

Transfigured high up mount, face shining sun,

Clothes brilliant light,*Lk 9:28* aside Moses, 'Lijah,

God's deliverer and revered prophet,

Speaking with the Son,*Mk 9:4* not idle talk but

Son to die in Jerusalem, horrible

But magnificent sacrifice for man,*Lk 9:31*

God revealing hidden things, created

New so that you cannot say you knew them,*Isa 48:6*

Keeping you on his straight and narrow path,

Off the many broad paths to destruction,*Matt 7:13*

For a highway called Way of Holiness

Will be there for those who walk on that Way,*Isa 35:8*

Father saving as many as desire,

But few choosing the Son's only rescue,*Lk 13:22*

Striving to work their way in, not poss'ble,*Ro 9:30*

None but Son good enough to qualify.*Gal 3:11*

The Son's transfiguration dumbfounded

The helpless disciples, shocked what to say,*Mk 9:5*

Dreamlike but awake, real rather vision,*Lk 9:32*

Ending bright cloud, Father proclamation,

The Father loved the Son who pleased Father,*Matt 17:5*

Disciples falling face down in terror,

To cower until Son's comforting touch,*Matt 17:6*

Secret to retain 'til Son rise from dead,*Matt 17:9*

Disciples yet conceive event's meaning,*Mk 9:10*

Transfiguration concealed in their hearts,*Lk 9:36*

Like Moses descending from Sinai mount,

> Knowing not his face shone, God encounter,*Exo 34:29*

God's glory descended on meeting tent,

> That Moses not enter tabernacle,*Exo 40:35*

Martyr Stephen transfigured stoning, too,

> Condemning council seeing angel's face.*Acts 6:15*

You cannot repay Father for wrong done;*Heb 10:1*

> Trying forever, clean yourself, won't work,*Heb 10:2*

More trying, more learning how much you owe,*Heb 10:3*

> Son paying only hope, owing too much,*Heb 10:4*

Trying and again, never measure up,*Heb 10:11*

> Yet the Son's one payment more than enough,*Heb 9:25*

The transfigured doing your transforming,

> Full, forever, magnif'cent paradise.

Book 7: Rejection

Opposed

Son must face horrific opposition

　　To complete his Father's salvation plan,

Submit to sacrifice at human hands,

　　Opposition starting from first grand work,

In Son's own hometown, reading Isaiah,*Lk 4:16*

　　Foretelling good news, reader Son fulfilled,*Lk 4:21*

People in darkness, seeing Son's great light,*Isa 9:2*

　　Yokes shattered,*Isa 9:4* all battles won,*Isa 9:5*

For a child born, Son of Father given,

　　All government on the one child's shoulders,

This Jesus whom they knew, Almighty God,

　　Yes, Prince of Peace, Everlasting Father,*Isa 9:6*

Whose government and peace would never end,

　　Reigning with justice and peace forever,*Isa 9:7*

So to man God says away with song,*Amos 5:23* but

　　Justice roll in never-ending rivers.*Amos 5:24*

Ask Son for greater faith in this gospel,*Lk 17:5*

　　Looking forward better place, not leaving,*Heb 11:14*

Faith giving back your dead, living again,*Heb 11:35*

 Enduring torture, jeers, lashing, prison,*Heb 11:35*

Facing worst death, dressed in tatters, dest'tute,*Heb 11:37*

 Holding on as Father holds onto you.*Heb 10:23*

The Son's gracious words amazed his hometown,

 Reminded merely neighbor Joseph's son,*Lk 4:22*

To no good, rejecting words for wonders,

 Not 'bout to honor Son, no less worship,*Lk 4:23*

Though the Father sent Elijah to help,

 He wearing hair garment and leather belt,*2Kings 1:8*

Calling the fire of God down from heaven,*2Kings 1:14*

 As the Son came to likewise help others,

But people reject whomever God sends,*Lk 4:25*

 Son's words making ev'ryone furious,*Lk 4:28*

Those who knew his mother, brothers, sisters,

 Offended at him who had no training,*Matt 13:54*

Like Bikri's Sheba deserting David,

 Trumpet sound to call Israel 'gainst their king,*2Sam 20:1*

Like scoundrels surrounding Solomon's son

 Rehoboam when still too weak and young,*2Chron 13:7*

Like Jeroboam,*1Kings 11:26* Zimri,*1Kings 16:20* rebellions,

 Babylon opposing the Lord at cost,*Jer 50:24*

Like Noah boarding Joppa ship toward

 Tarshish, fleeing from Lord in vi'lent storm.*Jonah 1:3*

The Son saw their lack of faith, giving him

 No honor, though their own eyes saw, ears heard,

He had no wonders nor healing for them,

Faith before gift for the hard hearted,*Mk 6:4*

Murd'rous people driving Son to cliff's edge,

Son walking right through them on message way.*Lk 4:29*

Don't presume yourself the Father's darling,

But serve others humbly like the Son did,*Matt 20:20*

When opposed, trying to lead quiet life,

Minding your own bus'ness, working with hands,*1Th 4:11*

Humiliation proving diligence,*Jas 1:9*

Others getting credit that you deserve,*2Co 12:11*

Looking only for Father's approval,*2Co 10:18*

No more putting yourself above others,*Php 2:3*

Learning quietly, without giving in,*1Ti 2:11*

Not puffing yourself up over others,*1Co 4:6*

Learning the Son's gentle, humble manner,*Matt 11:29*

Especially when vig'rously opposed,

Like Elisha let God send bears to maul

Boys who heckled the old baldy prophet.*2Kings 2:23*

Disciples grumbled over Son teaching

That he is bread of life, whose flesh to eat,

Whose blood to drink, too lit'rally taken,*Jn 6:60*

Many rejecting, opposing, leaving,*Jn 6:66*

Half brothers, sons of Joseph and Mary,

Rejecting him over his secrecy,*Jn 7:2*

When the Son's time was not yet,

Anytime others, but Son, Father 'wait,

The world hating only the Son because

He showed the world filled itself with evil.*Jn 7:6*

Pharisees challenged the Son, too, saying

> He could not speak for himself, but the Son

Pointed them to his Father's words, showing

> That they did not know him or his Father,Jn 8:13

Pharisees throwing from the synagogue

> Any who thought of following the Son,Jn 9:22

Temple Jews wondering if Son Savior,

> Son saying so to the disbelieving,Jn 10:22

Rule-keepers who flaunted their corruption,

> Killing, lusting, enslaving, and lying,1Ti 1:8

Every do-not becoming a do,Ro 7:8

> Their bodies urging them to break all rules,Ro 7:23

Sowing the wind to reap the whirlwind,

> Their stalks without heads, producing no flour,Hosea 8:7

Man in his rebel nature on display,

> Still son of Adam, not due Son of Man.

Divided

Some opposed the Son, others followed him,

> Dividing people wherever he went,

Some saying good, others that he deceived,

> All fearing the leaders, who hated him,Jn 7:12

Divided like the earth in Peleg's time,Gen 10:25

> Ahab, Obadiah divided land,1Kings 18:6

Israel, Judah divided promised land,Ezek 37:22

> Daniel divided Medes and Persians land.Dan 5:28

Many took Son's miracles as ev'dence,

> Why leaders sent guards to arrest the Son,*Jn 7:31*

Crowds divided, if causeless rebel or

> Bethlehem Savior, as scriptures foretold,*Jn 7:40*

Old rules showing the Savior coming,*Heb 10:1*

> Showing that you need Father's help saving,*Heb 7:18*

Preparing you to rely on the Son,*Heb 8:5*

> Sacrifices insufficient to pay.*Heb 10:8*

Yet division worsened when guards failed to

> Arrest the Son because he spoke like none,*Jn 7:45*

Leaders retorting Son had 'gain deceived,

> Only accursed mob accepting Son.*Jn 7:45*

Council member Nic'demus sought spare Son,

> But council no Gal'lean prophet knew,*Jn 7:50*

Leaving only masses following Son

> Who to them confirmed he was God's One.*Jn 8:25*

Hard man finds to worship Father in peace,*1Ti 2:8*

> Without quarrel, ruining listeners,*2Ti 2:14*

Useless controversy and arguments,*Tit 3:9*

> Desires fueling divide, battling within,*Jas 4:1*

When Father wants you asking what you want,*Jas 4:2*

> Without your grumbling or your argument,*Php 2:14*

Reviling thoughts, bedroom curses carried

> On little bird's wings to king for report,*Ecc 10:20*

Nor teachers divide, what learned, who followed,*1Co 3:4*

> Just make sound judgments relying on Son,*1Co 6:2*

Avoiding provoking, and have no conceit,*Gal 5:26*

Because disputes destroy one another,*Gal 5:15*

So keep issues between you and Father,*Php 3:15*

Warning the disruptive,*1Th 5:14* keeping away.*Th 3:6*

The Son's healing just worsened the divide,

Officials saying wrong day, no Father,

When no ord'nary one give sight to blind,*Jn 9:16*

But the officials threw out the healed man,*Jn 9:28*

Who knew the healer Jesus was the One,*Jn 9:35*

People still divided, calling him crazed,

While some said no crazed man opened blind eyes,*Jn 10:19*

Some accepting him, others rejecting,

Leaders who accepted keeping silent,

Caring more for here and now than after.*Jn 12:39*

Derided

People also derided, mocked the Son,

Despising him as one from whom people

Hide their faces, holding him in such shame,*Isa 54:3*

Drunkard, glutton they called him, for eating

With workers, tax agents, the ord'nary,*Matt 11:19*

Religious leaders sneering at the Son

When he criticized their love of money,*Lk 16:14*

Law teachers calling the Son blasphemer

For forgiving a paralyzed man healed,*Lk 5:21*

Grumbling 'gainst Son for saying he could feed

From his body,*Jn 6:51* when he thousands did so,*Matt 14:21*

To them, Joseph's uneducated son,*Jn 6:41*

Even his own family members calling him crazed,

   Incompetent, seeking his caretake charge,*Mk 3:21*

Taking God's place, as people gathered to

   Build Babel's tower, making their own way

To heaven,*Gen 11:4* rather than await Son's way,

   So that God must confuse and scatter them.*Gen 11:7*

Watch that none deceive, claiming be the Son;*Mk 13:5*

   No deceiving children, better to drown,*Lk 17:1*

Better not get truth wrong,*Lk 7:23* devour the weak,*Mk 12:38*

   Or mislead seekers,*Lk 11:52* rather avoid all

Deception, rejecting the enemy,*1Ti 4:1*

   Never perverting good news,*Gal 1:7* always true,*1Pe 2:1*

Never exploiting fantasies,*1Pe 2:3* never

   Arguing just to argue,*1Ti 6:4-5* deceptive,*2Ti 3:13*

Never rejecting Father to speak lies,

   Everything those touch coming to ruin,*Ro 2:13*

Their prophets' visions worthless because they

   Did not expose sin, warding off capture,*Lam 2:14*

Did not examine the people's ways to

   Test those ways to quick return to the Lord.*Lam 3:40*

No matter Son's wonders, people laughed

   In scorn at synagogue leader Jairus

Asking Son to bring dead daughter to life,*Lk 8:53*

   Leaders saying the Son's demons worked for

Satan, perfect Man called wholly devil,*Matt 9:34*

   Law teachers say Son had dirty spirit,*Mk 3:29*

While Son warned some would devour disciples,*Lk 10:3*

    Refusing them welcome, saying get lost,*Lk 9:51*

So James and John asked if holy fire should

    Rain on opponents, but Son just walked on.*Lk 9:54*

Son and disciples faced such derision

    That they found hard, finding places to rest,

So that when a man said he would follow

    Son anywhere, Son said he'd get no rest.*Lk 9:57*

Some stop at nothing to oppose the Son,*Mk 3:1*

    Others furious at talk of the Son,*Lk 6:11*

Some opposing fiercely those loving Son,*Lk 11:53-54*

    All to ignore, for making their own mess.*Tit 1:10-11*

Pharisees and law teachers nonetheless prodded, poked,

    Demanding more wonders the Son refused,*Mk 7:12*

Calling them wicked and adulterous,

    Refusing entertaining miracles.*Matt 16:1*

Chief priests discouraged children in Son praise,

    Though scripture foretold children would love him;*Matt 21:15*

Law teachers nitpicked his every word,*Mk 12:13*

    Besieging the Son with their trick questions.*Lk 11:53*

Pharisees said Herod wanted Son dead,

    But Son said he'd die in Jerusalem,*Lk 13:31*

Knowing others would judge him among worst,

    Just as the ancient prophesies foretold.*Lk 22:37*

Suffering

The Son expected suffering, telling

His disciples religious officials

Would soon have him killed, but not to worry,

Because the Father would resurrect him,*Matt 16:21*

Peter insisting the Son was wrong, but

Son knowing the Father's salvation plan*Mk 8:32*

That a disciple would betray the Son

For execution 'fore resurrection.*Matt 17:22*

Son astonished and confused disciples

Who were afraid to ask what Son meant,*Lk 9:43*

But listen to the Son to know truth,*Jn 18:37*

Being sure that you hear him correctly,*Mk 4:9*

Considering carefully what you hear,*Mk 4:24*

Belonging to the Father when hearing,*Jn 8:47*

To listen to teaching better than to serve,*k 10:38*

The Father favoring all those who hear,*Lk 11:28*

Attending carefully to what you hear,

So as not to drift away from the truth,*Heb 2:1*

Listening before speaking,*Jas 1:19* holding tongue,*Jas 1:26*

Opening your heart wide when you do hear,*Eph 4:20*

As child listens to father's instruction,

And does not forsake mother's teaching.*Prov 1:8*

Son foretold Jerusalem death again,

To be condemned, mocked, flogged, and crucified,*Matt 20:17*

So scaring his disciples they nearly

Did not follow him to Jerusalem,*Mk 10:32*

Son hiding from the religious leaders

Who wanted to kill him,*Jn 7:1* people wond'ring

Why authorities even let him speak

Publicly when they wanted the Son dead,*Jn 7:25*

Son saying leaders knew Father sent him,

Leaders who tried even more to seize Son.*Jn 7:28*

The Father had spoken with leaders,*Heb 5:4*

Selected to represent the people,*Heb 5:1*

But religious officials are human,*Heb 5:2-3*

Mortal, corrupt, just like the rest of us,*Heb 7:23*

When the Son isn't mortal or corrupt,

Instead your one High Priest to rescue you,*Heb 7:28*

Offering himself rather than others,

As religious officials would offer,*Heb 8:3*

Chief Priest at once both human and divine,*Heb 8:2*

Uniquely yours, not representative,*Heb 7:26*

Who suffered worse than Job who lost his all,*Job 1:20*

Life ebbing away,*Job 30:16* days gripped in suff'ring,*Job 30:27*

Than Ezekiel laying on his side for

Four-hundred-thirty days iniquity,*Ezek 4:5*

Than Jeremiah beaten and in stocks,*Jer 20:2*

Cast into a cistern, sinking in mud,*Jer 38:6*

Than apostle Paul lashed, flogged, beaten, stoned,

Thrice shipwrecked, hungry, sleepless, and naked,*2Cor 11:23*

Son a man of suff'ring, familiar pain,*Isa 53:3*

Bearing our suff'ring, stricken, afflicted,*Isa 53:4*

God crushing him in suff'ring as off'ring

    For our iniquity, pay for our sin._Isa 53:10_

The Son said publicly they would kill him

    For what he said,_Jn 8:37_ he and Father are one,

Temple officials prepared to stone him,_Jn 10:30_

    Like officials elsewhere,_Jn 11:7_ threats effective,

Troubling Son to ask Father to save him,

    But yet come to suffer exactly so,_Jn 12:27_

Wanting last celebratory supper,_Lk 22:15_

    Ev'rything according to plan foretold._Acts 3:12_

So don't argue over who is greatest,_Mk 9:34_

    'Stead, last to be first, serving ev'ryone,_Mk 9:34_

Greatest least,_Lk 9:48_ not lording over others,

    Ruling only to serve, greatest youngest,_Lk 22:25_

God humbling braggart, honoring humble,_Matt 23:11_

    Son correcting arrogance,_1Co 4:18_ better love,_1Co 4:21_

Letting others tout you,_2Co 5:12_ no comparing,_2Co 10:12_

    Great suffering most to remain humble,_2Co 12:7_

First here, last there; last here, first with Father,_Matt 19:30_

    Proud getting humbling, humble getting praise._Lk 14:11_

The Son learned obedience from suff'ring,_Heb 5:8_

    Suff'ring simply perfecting his resolve,

As his suff'ring also perfected you,

    Become your source for living forever,_Heb 5:9_

The Son having done nothing at all wrong,

    Taking ev'ry insult,_1Pe 2:22_ suff'ring for you._1Ti 2:5_

Accusers, not followers, killed the Son,

And will stop you to silence the good news,*1Th 2:15*

So expect to suffer, but don't worry,

You'll have reward, while they get their deserved.

Plotting

Priests and elders wanted to kill the Son

To preserve their own power and privilege,

Using Sabbath healing as excuse to

Plot his death, for saying from the Father,*Jn 5:1*

What Son said or did hardly mattering,

Excuse for any reason to charge him,*Matt 12:10*

Purpose instead to rid the earth of him,*Matt 12:14*

Plotting e'en with government officials,*Mk 3:1*

Son's successes enraging the leaders,

Who hurried their plotting, anxious to kill,*Lk 6:11*

As Joseph's brothers plotted to kill him,*Gen 37:18*

Saul tried annihilate Gibeonites,*2Sam 21:5*

Ahab's Jezebel plotted 'gainst Naboth

To commandeer his coveted vineyard,*1Kings 21:7*

Balak plotted to destroy Israelites

Seeking Balaam's curse but getting proph'sy,*Num 22:40*

Iconium Jews and Gentiles plotted to

Stone the apostles Paul and Barnabas.*Acts 14:6*

Don't let others speak evil about good,*Ro 14:16*

Fool you into abandoning good news,*Gal 3:1*

So that your zeal becomes instead for them,*Gal 4:17*

125

Their cunning and craftiness roiling you,*Eph 4:14*

Fine-sounding arguments made to trick you,*Col 2:4*

Hollow and deceptive philosophy,*Col 2:8*

Idle notions, fantasies puffing up,*Col 2:18*

Impure motives and tricks appealing you,*1Th 2:3*

Flattery hiding greed,*1Th 2:5* promoting myths,*1Ti 4:7*

Making idle chatter,*1Ti 6:20* deceiving you.*1Co 15:33*

Fear of the Son's sway grew with growing crowds,

Leaders looking for new way to kill him,*Mk 11:18*

Hoping to arrest the Son before he

Embarrassed them further before the crowds,*Lk 20:19*

Wanting the Son dead because ev'ryone

Hung on his words, he also mocking them.*Lk 19:47*

When the Son asked why they tried to kill him,

The leaders called him deranged, denying,*Jn 7:19*

Until the Son brought Laz'rus back to life,

When the leaders approved his murder plot

So that no more would go over to him,

Destroying their money-making power.*Jn 11:46*

Teachers who deny the Son will suffer*Matt 23:13*

Because they are doing the devil's work,*Matt 23:15*

Doing little things while ignoring big,*Lk 11:42*

Making a show of work, hardly working,*Matt 23:24*

Looking good outwardly, ugly within,*Lk 11:39*

Working hard to look good, doing no good,*Lk 11:43*

Pretending God's honor, killing children,*Matt 23:29*

Opposing God's workers, getting their due.*Matt 23:33*

The leaders ordered to report the Son,*Jn 11:57*

Planning to kill Son's friend Laz'rus, too,*Jn 12:9*

But crowds just kept talking of Son's wonders,

Huge crowds greeting Son entering city,

Leaders' plot failing, all going to Son,*Jn 12:17*

Son telling all they would crucify him.*Matt 16:21*

Sharing good news exposes some to death,*2Co 11:24*

But don't we all face the same death sentence?*2Co 1:9*

Death works 'gainst you so that life works in you,*2Co 4:12*

Ev'rything death 'til you rely on Son,*2Co 2:16*

The enemy wanting to kill those who

Share the Son's good news, wanting death, not life.*Rev 2:13*

Anointing

The Son prepared for death and burial,

As Abr'am bought the cave of Machpelah,*Gen 23:20*

As Magi brought the child Messiah myrrh,*Matt 2:11*

Nicodemus brought myrrh for Son's body,*John 19:39*

The Son permitted a sinful woman

Bringing alabaster jar*Lk 7:37* to caress

His unwashed feet with her hair and tears,*Lk 7:38*

Pouring perfume o'er the Son, forgiven,*Lk 7:47*

While Son's Pharisee host hadn't loved much,*Lk 7:44*

Not having sensed great need for forgiveness,

Disciples complaining of perfume cost,

Son saying others would long remember.*Matt 26:6*

127

Friend Mary anointed Son with perfume,

    Wiped his feet with her hair at a dinner,_{Jn 12:1}

Betrayer Judas decrying the cost

    Because he was a thief stealing money,_{Jn 12:4}

The Son saying to leave Mary alone,

    Her perfume the cost of his burial,_{Jn 12:7}

The good news to long tell her love for him,

    Even preparing him for his burial._{Matt 26:12}

So shame on those who live for their comfort,_{Lk 6:24}

    Wealth choking good news,_{Matt 13:22} their greed on display,_{Lk 12:13}

The Father demanding their life tonight,_{Lk 12:16}

    Riches tempting and trapping to ruin,_{1Ti 6:9}

When you have enough, Father providing,_{Heb 13:5}

    Loving money distracting, depleting,_{1Ti 6:10}

Hoarding wealth courting coming misery,_{Jas 5:5}

    Cheating workers fattening for slaughter._{Jas 5:5}

Greed is ev'rywhere,_{1Co 5:10} worldly swindlers,_{1Co 5:10}

    Continual wrongs,_{1Pe 2:14} all pursuing riches,_{Matt 6:21}

Money lovers sneering at Son lovers,_{Lk 16:14}

    While coveting one another's riches,_{Acts 20:33}

Busying themselves in their paneled houses,_{Haggai 1:9}

    While the Lord's own house remains in ruins,_{Haggai 1:4}

Living in luxury, beggar Laz'rus

    At their gates on his way to the Father,

While the luxuriating end in hell,_{Lk 16:22}

    Getting not tongue-tip relief, then too late,_{Lk 16:24}

But the good news turns the swindlers around,_{1Co 6:9}

When everything is already yours.$_{1Co\ 3:21}$

Betrayal

The Son foretold his death by betrayal,

Though some disciples would not believe him;

He knew who would reject and betray him,

knowing man's heart and acts before we do,$_{Jn\ 6:64}$

Calling one of the twelve mischievous fiend,

Devil, Judas Iscariot, betrayer,$_{Jn\ 6:70}$

Giving the officials quiet arrest,$_{Matt\ 21:45}$

Son warning someone would hand him over$_{Matt\ 26:1}$

Secretly for his execution, so

Festival attendees wouldn't riot,$_{Mk\ 14:1}$

Officials still fearing the crowds he drew,$_{Lk\ 22:1}$

So glad wayward Judas would secret meet,

His Lord to betray in Satan's employ,$_{Lk\ 22:3}$

Loving money, at thirty-silver wage,$_{Matt\ 26:14}$

As Mosaic law priced slaves$_{Exo\ 21:32}$ and

Zechariah foretold that Israel

Would sell her detested Lord God shepherd,$_{Zech\ 11:12}$

To betray Son for their secret arrest,$_{Mk\ 14:11}$

Preferring shepherds who consume the flock

To the One who gave his life for their care;$_{Ezek\ 34:2}$

Oh, Lord, shepherd the flock marked for slaughter!$_{Zech\ 11:4}$

'Specially the oppressed of the flock.$_{Zech\ 11:7}$

Be careful that carousing not corrupt,$_{Lk\ 21:34}$

Indulging only 'til you learn better,*Eph 2:3*

Once natural before realizing loss,*Ro 7:5*

Desire still present, pursuit optional,*Gal 5:19*

The indulgent enticing others join,*1Pe 2:18*

Promising freedom while making a slave,*1Pe 2:19*

Led from Father,*Ro 8:7* no effort to control,*Col 2:13*

Father releasing to degrade body,*Ro 1:24*

Shameful lusts flourishing, leading to death,*Ro 1:26*

Only the Spirit stopping indulgence.*Col 2:23*

The Son supped late last with his disciples,

Foretelling 'gain that one would betray him,*Jn 13:21*

One dipping his hand in their common bowl*Lk 22:21*

And taking Son's bread offer from his hand,*Jn 13:25*

Foretold one sharing bread would betray him,*Jn 13:18*

Judas asking him, Son replying so,*Matt 26:24*

That moment Satan seized Judas,*Jn 13:26* quickly,

Son said to do,*Jn 13:26* Judas leaving in dark,*Jn 13:30*

Like Cain killing Abel o'er Lord's favor,

When he was indeed his brother's keeper,*Gen 4:9*

Like servant Ziba betraying master

Mephibosheth, slandered before lord,*2Sam 19:26*

The treacherous betray!*Isa 24:16* woe to betray,*Isa 33:1*

Family betraying,*Jer 12:6* friends betraying,*Lam 1:2*

Yet Son assuring only one betray,*Jn 13:10*

Before disciples see Son again,*Jn 16:16*

Disciples very glad of his return,

So glad no one would take away their joy.*Jn 16:21*

Salvation pure, rejection corruption,*Tit 1:15*

Actions proving fitness or for nothing,*Tit 1:16*

So live not in futil'ty like others,*Eph 4:17*

Hardened and darkened in your ignorance,*Eph 4:18*

Losing all sensitivity, impure,*Eph 4:19*

Suiting desires, hearing only wanted,*2Ti 4:3*

Turning from truth to myth,*2Ti 4:4* deserting taught,*2Ti 4:10*

Justice due, corrupt finding no relief.*Rev 21:8*

The Son's foretelling confirmed who he was,*Jn 13:19*

Father's plan, though Judas better not born,*Matt 26:24*

Trying to return paid silver, too late,

To mean priests blaming him for their own plot,*Matt 27:3*

So threw their silver into the Temple,

To hang himself,*Matt 27:5* priests' blood money buying

Potter's field for dead strangers, as foretold,*Matt 27:6*

As Peter later preached Son's fulfillment.*Acts 1:16*

Wrongdoing, and paying, pleased not God,*Heb 10:8*

So Son set 'side old trade for new, all paid,*Heb 10:9*

Bonus to live forever free and new,*Heb 8:6*

Now out of your spiritual slavery,*Heb 8:9*

New making old outdated, obsolete,*Heb 8:13*

New heart, new mind, no longer breaking rules,*Heb 8:10*

Wanting to do as the Father commands,*Heb 10:16*

The Father's Spirit in you, your conscience.*2Co 1:22*

The Son broke last bread for the disciples

To eat as his body,*Matt 26:26* poured last wine to

Drink as his blood, forgiven corruption,*Mk 14:23*

Both new promises of his death for you,*Lk 22:20*

Sacrament by which to remember him,*ICo 11:23*

    Oft to eat his body and drink his blood,*ICo 11:25*

Sharing the Son's death,*ICo 10:16* whenever said done,*ICo 11:26*

    Spiritual food and drink as others have,*ICo 10:3*

Genuine life forever,*Jn 6:52* Son alive,*Jn 6:56*

    Together, respectfully,*ICo 11:20* examined,*ICo 11:28*

Giving careful thought to one's ways,*Haggai 1:5* going

    Up for mountain timbers to build God's house,*Haggai 1:8*

The enemy his cup thank not to drink,*ICo 10:21*

    Instead relying fully on the Son.*ICo 11:27*

Garden

The last betrayal was in Gethsem'ne

    Garden, Son's fav'rite place for prayer and rest,

There after last supper to pray Father,*Matt 26:36*

    Telling his disciples to pray, too, that

They not to temptation fall like Judas,*Lk 22:40*

    Then taking Peter, James, and John aside,

As deathly sorrow overwhelmed the Son,*Matt 26:37*

    Pray! Watch and pray in Son's needful dark hour!

While Son stone's throw kneeled, praying to Father,*Lk 22:41*

    Facedown to ask relieve him of duty,

But then Father's will to do, no wishing,*Mk 14:35*

    Father sent an angel to strengthen Son,*Lk 22:43*

While Son prayed in ever greater anguish,

Sweat falling furrowed brow as drops of blood,*Lk 22:44*

But finding trusted disciples sleeping,*Matt 26:40*

Sorrow exhausted,*Lk 22:45* just to watch one hour!*Mk 14:37*

Son begged rise, watch, pray, lest Satan tempted,*Matt 26:41*

Their spirit willing but flesh weak,*Mk 14:38* again

Son went 'side to pray, while disciples sleep,*Matt 26:42*

Third time the same, but then to sudden rise,

Hour having come for betrayer Judas

To deliver Son in enemy's hands.*Mk 14:41*

You, worry not what to say in trials,

The Spirit instead giving you his voice,*Mk 13:11*

Words adversaries cannot contradict,*Lk 21:14*

Like martyr Stephen speaking Spirit words,*Acts 6:8*

Strong, fighting unlike weak others must fight,*Lk 22:35*

Strong in Father's power,*Eph 6:10* truth on to stand,*Eph 6:14*

Like youth David relying on the Lord

In battle with enormous Goliath,*1Samuel 17:4*

Enduring,*Col 1:10* no trial unsettling you,*1Th 3:3*

Remembering faith others have in you.*1Ti 1:18*

Book 8: Execution

Arrest

The Son's execution took but a day,

    Without due process, evil does not wait.

Betrayer Judas knew Gethsemane,

    Where Son and his disciples often met,*Jn 18:2*

So there he led large armed crowd priests had sent.*Matt 26:47*

    Soldiers, officials accompanied crowd,

Carrying their torches, weapons, lanterns,*Jn 18:3*

    Son knowing what would happen, in control,

Out to ask whom they wanted,*Jn 18:4* he, the Son!

    His captors fell back awestruck to the ground,*Jn 18:5*

Their approach bringing them to holy mound,

    To let the others go, as Son command,

That he would lose none, as prayed,*Jn 17:9* and foretold,*Jn 6:39*

    No worries, the Son returning for you,

Your special place he prepared in his home,*Jn 14:1*

    To which you know the way: only through him,*Jn 14:4*

Son giving his peace, not worldly but real,*Jn 14:27*

    The Father comforting you in trouble,*2Co 1:4*

You sharing some of the Son's suffering,

But enjoying all of the Son's comfort.2Co 1:5

Judas had a signal for Son's arrest,

A kiss, of all things, straight to Son to greet,

Son noting ugly irony, asking

Judas if his kiss would betray the Son,Lk 22:47

Adding to do that for which Judas came,Matt 26:48

As others stepped forward, make Son's arrest.Matt 26:50

Impulsive Peter drew sword, sev'ring high

Priest servant Malchus' ear,Lk 22:49 Son command cease,

To do as God granted, arrest and death;Jn 18:11

Sheathe your swords by which you live and die,

Let Son call angel legions if he wished,

But here as foretold submit to mission,Matt 26:52

Because the enemy has no power,Jn 19:10

Son overthrow,2Th 2:7 temptation his only,Ro 2:8-11

Deception aided,2Th 2:9 Father permitting

Powerful delusion, to reject Son.2Th 2:11

Struggle then not with health but deception,Eph 6:12

Son disarming other en'my power.Col 2:15

The Son healed the servant's ear with grace touch,Lk 22:51

No rebel but open, public, having

Taught Temple the same at Jerusalem,Matt 26:55

But darkness was his captors' shameful hour,Lk 22:53

So at official behest, soldiers bound

Glory King, treated as common crim'nal,Jn 18:12

Disciples fleeing for their nat'ral lives,Mk 14:50

Young man fleeing naked, seized robe left behind.*Mk 14:51*

Satan killed the Son, yet no vict'ry won,

    Proving only Son gives all for Father,*Jn 14:30*

The enemy murderer, sure liar,*Jn 8:44*

    Wanting you lying, too,*Jn 8:44* costing you all,*Acts 5:1-6*

Laying in wait to destroy any fool,*1Pe 5:8*

    Let not that be you,*Jas 2:19* Son's words stop devil,*2Ti 2:25*

But underestimate this Satan not,

    His subtle deception,*2Th 2:9* hate to indulge,*1Jn 3:9*

Envy, selfishness,*Jas 3:14-16* tormenting body,

    Though never spirit,*2Co 12:7* God's Spirit protects,*1Ti 4:1*

Good reputation inoculation,*1Ti 3:7*

    Doing Father's work,*1Co 10:20* Son prayed protection,*Lk 22:31*

So rivers through which you pass not sweep

    You away, nor fires walk through set aflame,*Isa 43:2*

For surely Jesus is the Lord your God,

    Holy One of Israel, your sure Savior.*Isa 43:3*

Trial

Nighttime trial followed, not real, charade,

    All knowing the outcome before started,

Though Torah law required one accused

    Stand fair trial before the assembly,*Num 35:12*

As God will judge all nations fairly in

    Jehosaphat's Valley, for scattering

His people Israel among the nations

While dividing up his land for themselves,*Joel 3:2*

As God Almighty puts all on trial,

Quick to judge those who oppress the widow.*Mal 3:5*

Here, high priest Annas questioned Son sharply,*Jn 18:19*

Son saying he taught only openly,*Jn 18:21*

Official's slap he drew for truth he spoke,*Jn 18:22*

Sending him to next high priest Caiaphas,

Who had said Son must die for the people,*Jn 18:13*

As the Son indeed did die, though Savior.

The Son stood alone before Sanhedrin,*Matt 26:57*

John quiet aside,*Jn 18:15* Peter in courtyard,*Jn 18:16*

Talking with servant girl, sitting with guards,*Mk 14:54*

Priests waiting for false ev'dence to convict,*Matt 26:59*

False witnesses many, evidence none,*Mk 14:56*

Even false testimony differing.*Mk 14:58*

Many leave the Son over hard teaching,*Jn 6:60*

But where have you to go beyond the Son?*Jn 6:67*

Lapse in hardship, yes, but then just return,*Matt 26:31*

All abandoning the Son at some point,*Jn 16:31*

But the Son prayed to keep and restore you,*Lk 22:31*

Even though you are not especially brave;*Mk 14:29*

Son's the committed one; rely on him*Matt 26:35*

To get back on track rather than regret.*Lk 22:62*

Caiaphas demanded the Son answer,

To no avail,*Matt 26:61* charging Son as Savior,*Mk 14:61*

All joining in, demanding Son respond,

Knowing who Son but refuse to admit.*Lk 22:66*

137

The Son finally replied they would not

    Believe him_Lk 22:67_ but he was indeed Savior;_Mk 14:62_

They would see the Son at his Father's side,

    Coming down from above as their ruler._Matt 26:64_

Caiaphas tore robe in angry judgment,

    Saying Sanhedrin needed no ev'dence;

They would convict the Son for his own words,

    Claiming author'ty they refused submit._Mk 14:63_

Spit they then in Son's face, struck, slapped, and mocked,_Matt 26:66_

    Blindfolded for his guards to mock and beat._Mk 14:65_

As beating continued, priests planned his death,

    Guards leading bound to governor Pilate._Matt 27:1_

Your struggle isn't truly 'gainst hunger and lust,

    But the en'my who influences you;_Eph 6:12_

So no distraction: focus on the Son;_Matt 6:22_

    The enemy runs when you resist,_Jas 4:7_ so

Leave the fight to your Father who's stronger;_Jude 8_

    You're no diff'rent, all in the same battle._1Pe 5:9_

Anger is en'my foothold, so stop it,_Eph 4:27_

    Careful with your en'my always present;_Eph 5:15_

While the Father crushes your enemy,_Ro 16:20_

    Foolish people still do his ugly work,_Matt 13:36_

Though the enemy ends up with nothing,_Matt 13:40-43_

    Because you're saved even if he kills you,

Son's royal paradise awaiting you,_Rev 2:9_

    Fully saved when relying on the Son._Rev 2:13_

Sentence

Early that morning, the priests paraded Son

   'Fore Roman governor Pontius Pilate,

Outside his palace, pretending pur'ty,

   But exhib'ting entire hypocrisy,*Jn 18:28*

Refusing even to tell the charges,*Jn 18:29*

   Like priests demanding Jeremiah die

For prophesying Jerusalem's fall,*Jer 26:11*

   But unable to execute Son without

Governor's consent,*Jn 18:31* who examined Son,*Jn 18:33*

   If he their Messiah, Son saying said,*Matt 27:11*

Pilate then asking why handed over,

   Son replying his otherworldly rule,*Jn 18:35*

That he had come to share truth and good news,*Jn 18:37*

   Pilate sneering but finding no charges.*Jn 18:38*

Truth indeed exists only in the Son;

   Rely on what the Son says, always true,*1Ti 6:3*

The harder someone argues against Son,

   The harder you and others oppose them.*2Ti 4:15*

The priests charged the Son claimed to be ruler,*Mk 15:1*

   Son still silent to Pilate's amazement,*Matt 27:13*

So Pilate sent Son to Galilean

   Ruler Herod who hoped to see magic,*Lk 23:6*

But Son said nothing to corrupt ruler,*Lk 23:9*

   Who sent the Son back in elegant robe.*Lk 23:11*

Pilate said he'd punish and release Son,

But now crowd shouted to crucify him.*Lk 23:13*

Pilate released notor'ous Barrabas

As crowd demanded, 'stead of perfect One,*Matt 27:15*

Though Pilate's wife warned not to mistreat

Innocent Son, as hard dream informed her.*Matt 27:19*

Pilate washed hands of innocent Son's blood,*Matt 27:23*

The crowd agreeing Son's blood was on them,*Matt 27:25*

To have Son flogged and sent for cruc'fixion,*Jn 19:1*

The enemy doing his deadly work,*Matt 12:25*

Lifted up, appallingly disfigured,

Marred beyond man's likeness, Isaiah foretold,*Isa 52:13*

Grown without beauty or majesty,*Isa 53:2* Son

Despised, rejected, bearing our suff'ring,*Isa 53:3*

Pierced for our trangressions, crushed for our sin,*Isa 53:5*

Led silent like a lamb to its slaughter,*Isa 53:7*

Though without fault, assigned the wicked's grave,*Isa 53:9*

Our punishment and healing upon him,*Isa 53:5*

The Lord's will to crush him in full torment,

His life, the perfect off'ring for our sin.*Isa 53:10*

Satan is never good, always evil;*Lk 11:19*

Banish him,*Mk 3:27* replacing with Spirit friend.*Matt 12:43*

Others will call you evil,*Matt 11:18* when your good

Work exposes and threatens their bad work.*Jn 7:19*

Reject Son, and you follow the en'my,*Jn 8:39*

But accept Son, and the en'my submits.*Acts 19:13*

Soldiers stripped and robed the Son, jamming thorned

Crown, putting staff in hand, and mock kneeling,

140

While spitting on him, striking him with staff,

    Cruelly, as the people's supposed king.*Matt 27:27*

Pilate repeated the Son met no charge,

    But priests shouted again crucify One

Who claimed to be Father's Son, who must die,

    Pilate more afraid he would kill a king,*Jn 19:4*

Questioning 'gain, Son still not answering,*Jn 19:9*

    'Til Pilate crucifixion power claimed,

When Son said governor's only power

    Was from God above,*Jn 19:10* Pilate trying free

Son, priests saying Caesar demanded death,*Jn 19:12*

    Pilate offering Son as their ruler,*Jn 19:14*

Priests replying Caesar alone ruled them!*Jn 19:15*

    Given up their own God for earthly king,

Preferring despot rule preserve power,

    'Til Pilate handed over Son to die,*Jn 19:16*

Like Ahab king of Israel condemning

    Himself when passing a prophet's sentence.*1Kings 20:40*

The Son's word exposed, beat the enemy,*Matt 4:3*

    Who knows Son's premier status, as should you,*Mk 3:11*

Son having seen Father throw out en'my,*Lk 10:18*

    Beaten back so that you could step forward,*Jn 12:30-32*

Son making spectacle of the en'my,*Col 2:15*

    Son and en'my having nothing common,*2Co 6:15*

You having to choose one side or other,*1Co 10:21*

    Not letting enemy befriend fool you.*2Co 11:3*

The Son made himself like you to come back

After en'my death, to give you new life,*Heb 2:14*

You to do what you see the Son doing,*1Jn 3:7*

The Son serving you, though en'my doesn't.*Ro 8:38*

Crucifixion

They killed the Son by most hideous means,

As prophesy foretold before invented,

Bashan's bulls circling Son, piercing hands, feet,*Psa 22:16*

To stare and gloat over bones on display.*Psa 22:17*

Son carried cross toward stony outcrop Skull,*Jn 19:16*

'Long via Dolorosa, sorrow's way,

Cross stations marked, 'til Son cross couldn't bear,

Guards 'stead forcing Simon the Cyrene,*Matt 27:32*

Women following, mourning and wailing,

Though Son saying weep for selves and children.*Lk 23:27*

Soldiers offered sedative drink, refused,*Mk 15:23*

Then stripped the Son, nailing hard gospel cross,

As he prayed forgive, casting clothing lots,*Mk 15:24*

His garment undivided, as foretold.*Psa 22:18*

Ask that Father forgive your many wrongs,*Matt 6:12*

Humbling yourself as you ask, not on pride,*Lk 18:14*

Asking forgiveness for others, also,*Jas 5:13*

All those relying on forgiving Son.*1Jn 5:16*

Pilate's cross sign named the Son the Jew's king,*Matt 27:34*

Over priest protest, having so written,*Jn 19:21-22*

In three tongues many passersby could read,*Jn 19:19*

Crucifying with Son two criminals,*Matt 27:38*

Mocking and insulting Son for claim to

Rebuild Temple, unable to save self.*Mk 15:29*

One criminal, though, rebuked the other,

Saying that the Son had done nothing wrong,*Lk 23:39*

Asking the Son to please remember him,

Son reply together have paradise.*Lk 23:42*

Mother and aunt wept with other women,

As Son died above them, lifted on tree,*Jn 19:25*

Son telling John to care for Son's mother,*Jn 19:26*

Serving, thoughtful, forging to the last.

Thus did officials kill the perfect Man,*1Co 2:8*

Yet the Son living by Father's power,*2Co 13:4*

Defeating ev'ry contrary power,*Col 2:15*

Suffering ignominy for honor,*Heb 12:2*

To bring everything back together,*Eph 2:15*

Through extr'ord'nary act dying on cross.*Col 1:20*

Become vict'ry symbol, as Moses snake

Lifted on pole*Num 21:8* to heal bitten people,*Jn 3:14*

As Son foretold he would draw all to him,*Jn 12:32*

After three days dead,*Matt 12:40* like Jonah in whale,*Jonah 1:17*

Debt nailed to cross,*Col 2:14* vict'ry over evil,*Col 2:15*

Crucifying ev'rything but the Son,*Gal 6:14*

Foolishness to those who will die, power

Over death for those who on Son rely.*1Co 1:18*

Death

Darkness fell midday, while Son on cross lived,

　　Sun hiding as the Father turned away,_{Mk 15:33}

Son crying in anguish, Father withdrawn,

　　As Father must turn from sin Son assumed,_{Matt 27:46}

Those watching thinking Son called a prophet,

　　When he talked only to his one Father._{Mk 15:35}

Knowing accomplished, Son admitted thirst,_{Jn 19:28}

　　For vinegar sponge held on staff aloft,_{Matt 27:48}

All watching for prophet to take Son down,_{Mk 15:36}

　　Though Son bowed head, saying his work was done._{Jn 19:30}

Last breath gasped,_{Matt 27:50} Spirit committed Father

　　Again, whom Son would resurrected join._{Lk 23:46}

Son's death moment cataclysmic occurred,

　　Great Temple curtain torn open for all,_{Matt 27:51}

Earthquake, tombs broken open, prophets rose,_{Matt 27:51}

　　Centurion exclaiming Son Savior died,_{Matt 27:54}

Perfectly good man now dead,_{Lk 23:47} slink away,_{Lk 23:48}

　　Caring women_{Matt 27:55} and disciples distance watched._{Lk 23:49}

The priests still thought of ritual duty,

　　No bodies on Sabbath crosses to see,

So asked of Pilate their legs to break to

　　Ensure swift death before the Sabbath dawn,_{Jn 19:31}

Soldiers breaking crim'nals' but not Son's legs,_{Jn 19:32}

　　Instead, soldier pierced dead Son's side with spear,

Bloody fluid from Son pouring, foretold,

No broken bones but on pierced they would look,*Jn 19:34*

For Peter later to courageously

Proclaim officials killed Son on the cross.*Acts 10:39*

Father gave Son's life for all that you owed,*Ro 2:25*

To die in your place, as you should have died,*Ro 4:25*

His love, that you turn from your brokenness,*2Co 5:14*

Your old mess so that you can live with Son life,*Gal 2:20*

No fancy theory out of cross power,*1Co 1:17*

But share cup relying wholly on Son,*1Co 10:16*

Who made spotless for riches undeserved,*Eph 1:7*

So to tell this good news with simple words,*1Co 2:1*

Some wanting wonders, others philos'phy,

But you only gospel drawn from Father.*1Co 1:22*

The Son died as Abel died, bringing God

His better firstfruit blood offering,*Heb 11:4*

Noah died, righteousness's heir building

Ark for humankind, from his lone sole faith,*Heb 11:7*

Abr'am died living in promised-land tents,*Heb 11:8*

Isaac and Jacob, heirs of same promise,*Heb 11:9*

Joseph died speaking of certain ex'dus,*Heb 11:22*

Moses died saving people, no reward,*Heb 11:24*

As countless other faith heroes died, too,

Relying on God's greater Son promise,*Heb 11:40*

For all, without Son, die, even oldest

Methuselah, nine hundred sixty nine.*Gen 5:27*

Burial

Proper burial Son would have, behest

    Arimathean Joseph, council he,

Having objected to Son's night trial,

    Seeing Son as was, Savior and ruler,

Joseph went boldly Pilate for body,*Matt 27:57*

    Belief no longer secret, now Son dead,

Council fear gone, ready for bold action,*Jn 19:38*

    Pilate his request granted, body his.*Mk 15:44*

The Son had to die, your blood to repay,

    How generous your Father was to you!*Eph 1:7*

Animal blood not enough, no longer,*Heb 13:11*

    Son dying outside same gate, your Savior,*Heb 13:12*

Confident you, approach Father in Son,

    His death opening your new way,*Heb 10:19* the One.*1Co 1:30*

Nicodemus joined Joseph, Son's body

    To retrieve, prepare, and entomb, custom

Way embalmed of myrhh and aloes,*Jn 19:39* linen

    wrapped, in Joseph's tomb cut from garden rock,

Huge stone rolled across tiny tomb entrance,*Matt 27:58*

    Two women sitting opposite the tomb,*Mk 15:47*

Then home to prepare spices and perfume,

    Resting next day, as custom required,*Lk 23:56*

Pilate at priest request securing tomb,

    Lest body stolen to prove foretold rise,*Matt 27:62*

Sealed with heavy rope and heav'ly guarded,*Matt 27:65*

So Son died before you did aught for him,*Ro 5:6*

As your advocate earned with his own death,*1Ti 2:5*

    Doing the humanly impossible.*2Ti 1:10*

Where has your beloved gone, most beautiful?

    Which way did he go that you look for him?*Song 6:1*

All night long on my bed I searched for him

    Whom my heart loves, looked but did not find him,*Song 3:1*

Rising to go through city streets and squares,

    Searching for the One whom my heart so loves.*Song 3:2*

See the city become a prostitute,

    Murder where justice, righteousness once dwelled.*Isa 1:21*

Book 9: Restoration

Resurrection

The Son lived after death as he foretold,

 That although others would cruelly kill him,

The Father would promptly resurrect him.*Matt 16:21*

 When women went to tomb after Sabbath,

Earth shook, sky opened, and angel appeared,

 Shoving aside huge stone, sitting atop,*Matt 28:1*

Stunned guards shaking with such fear as if dead.*Matt 28:4*

 The women looked inside for Son's body,

While angel said he'd risen as foretold,

 Amazed women hurried to tell others,*Matt 28:5*

But Son stopped and greeted them as they fell

 To clasp his feet in elated worship,*Matt 28:9*

Son saying tell others to meet him in

 Galilee, his home region, by the lake.*Matt 28:10*

The guards reported to the priests, who paid

 Them to say disciples stole the body.*Matt 28:11*

Women told disciples who believed not,*Lk 24:9*

 Peter, though, running to the tomb, seeing

Cast-off linen strips and missing body,

    Still unable believe what happened.*Lk 24:12*

Accept, don't reject, the Son rose again,*1Co 15:12*

    For only those dying reject good news,*2Co 4:3*

Culture blinding those who reject the Son,*2Co 4:4*

    When you must reject worldly perspective,*2Co 5:16*

To accept what many witnesses saw,*Heb 2:3*

    As foretold, accompanying wonders,*Heb 2:4*

As Moses sang of his Lord's salvation,*Exo 15:2*

    David sang God's shield and horn salvation,*2Sam 22:3*

Man's salvation come lone out of Zion,*Psa 14:7*

    Spear, javelin, signaling salvation,*Psa 35:3*

Praise song, Isaiah recorded, surely

    God is our salvation, strength, and defense,*Isa 12:2*

Salvation his city's ramparts and walls,*Isa 26:1*

    Too small to restore only Jacob's tribes,

Rather Son's role: salvation to earth's ends,*Isa 49:6*

    Heavens vanishing, salvation fore'er,*Isa 51:6*

First nat'ral human living and dying,

    First supernat'ral dying and living,*1Co 15:45*

Spiritual superseding natural,*1Co 15:46*

    First nat'ral from dust, first supernat'ral

From the Father's gentle Holy Spirit,*1Co 15:47*

    Leaving choice to die or live forever,*1Co 15:48*

All beginning earthly, but all free to

    Embrace their Father's full spiritual form.*1Co 15:49*

You may choose not to die but to change form,*1Co 15:51*

Instantly, at the Father's chosen time,_{1Co 15:52}

Dead body eternal spiritual form,_{1Co 15:53}

Like the Son rose, defeating your own death,_{1Co 15:54}

Death only hurting when no other way,

But now to receive the Son's perfect form,_{1Co 15:55}

Like Jacob rolling well's stone, beautif'lly

Formed wife Rachel to receive in blessing._{Gen 29:10}

Women who had cared for Son brought spices

To the tomb to anoint his body,_{Mk 16:1} but

The tomb's huge stone had already rolled back,_{Lk 24:2}

Son's body no longer there to anoint,_{Lk 24:3}

Fear-stricken women 'stead seeing robed man,

Telling them not to fear, Son had risen!_{Mk 16:5}

Believe angel word, just as he told them!_{Mk 16:7}

The women bowed to two gleaming angels_{Lk 24:4}

Who asked why look for living among dead,

For the Son had risen just as he said,_{Lk 24:5}

Trembling and bewildered women then fled._{Mk 16:8}

Magdalene Mary went early to tomb,

Stone moved aside,_{Jn 20:1} running tell Peter and

John someone had removed the Lord's body,_{Jn 20:2}

Disciples confirming only linen

Remained,_{Jn 20:3} still unable to grasp risen._{Jn 20:8}

Magdalene wept outside the tomb until

Angels she saw inside, asking why cry,_{Jn 20:11}

Someone body has stolen, her reply,

But turning saw Son, failing recognize,_{Jn 20:13}

Asking her why cry,*Jn 20:15* calling her Mary,

    Teacher! she in amazement, joy replied.*Jn 20:16*

Because Father raised Son, Son cannot die,*Ro 6:9*

    Death defeated, immortality nigh,*2Ti 1:10*

Those dying with Son, living forever,*2Ti 2:11*

    Those without Son to earthly dust return,*1Co 15:48*

Father unchanging in life to the Son,*Heb 13:20*

    Your unchangeable promise 'ready won,*Heb 9:15*

Made perfect forever, good for Father,*Heb 10:14*

    The Son's great gift of living forever.*Ro 6:21*

Son rules with Father,*Heb 1:8* all else wearing out,*Heb 1:11*

    Father and Son remaining forever,*Heb 1:12*

All looking to Son as giver of life,*Jn. 6:40*

    Son sustaining all eternally his.*Jn 6:50*

Appearance

Risen Son showed himself alive to his

    Disciples many times o'er forty days,

Speaking always of his Father's kingdom,*Acts 1:3*

    Two disciples walking Emaus road,

Talking disconsolately of Son's death,

    When hidden Son suddenly walked with them,*Lk 24:13*

They sharing empty tomb's discovery,*Lk 24:17*

    Son calling them foolish for missing told,*Lk 24:25*

Reminding them of foretelling scriptures,

    Break bread, ident'ty suddenly disclosed,*Lk 24:28*

As God appeared to ninety-nine-year-old

  Abr'am, promising to make him fruitful,*Gen 17:2*

Appeared to Jacob, when from Esau fled,

  At Jabbok ford struggle, called Peniel,*Gen 32:30*

Again Beersheba to Egypt flight 'prove,*Gen 46:2*

  'Gain return from Paddan Aram,*Gen 35:9* at Luz,*Gen 48:3*

To Solomon, all offered, wisdom asked,*2Chron 1:7*

  Isaac, Moses, and others, appeared, too.

The Father promises eternal life

  On your professing eternal good news,*1Ti 6:12*

So keep saying so, despite others' scold,*2Ti 1:8*

  Your generous acts leading others won,*2Co 9:13*

Acceptance putting you right, profession

  Ensuring Son rescues you, relying,*Ro 10:10*

Holding tight, trusting Father,*Heb 10:23* giv'n Spirit,*Jn 4:13*

  Staying simple, knowing only the Son,*1Co 2:1*

Bold to share,*2Co 3:12* talking up Son,*2Co 4:13* city won,*Heb 11:16*

  Reaching the lost for their sure salvation,*Php 1:20*

No longer trusting in mere humans who

  Have but a breath in their lungs, no esteem.*Isa 2:22*

Emaus two hurried Jerusalem

  Return, to tell others Son sure risen,*Lk 24:33*

When Son 'gain appeared, standing among them,

  So shocking disciples, Son reassured.*Jn 20:19*

Disciples behind locked doors they had been,

  Hiding from officials, when Son appeared,*Jn 20:19*

Terrifying disciples, must not him,

But the Son showed them his pierced hands and feet,

Still thinking apparition, Son said touch,*Lk 24:37*

Showing hands and side wounds, he was alive!*Jn 20:20*

Disciples thought all then was Father's rule,

But Son said not yet, the time a secret.*Acts 1:6*

Don't worry how God brings you back to life,*Co 15:35*

Happens for seed-borne plants as for humans,*Jn 12:24*

Sown seed coming to life,*1Co 15:36* seed given form,*1Co 15:38*

Although humans, God's image, do differ,*1Co 15:39*

Coming back to life, your body first dies

But returns death unable,*1Co 15:42* special form,

Dying powerless, returned powerful,*1Co 15:43*

Transformed from natural to spiritual,*1Co 15:44*

Unconcerned with triv'al earthly matters,

In the nature of celestial being.*Matt 22:23*

To further convince his stunned disciples,

Son asked for broiled fish to gladly eat,*Lk 24:41*

Reminding them meanwhile scriptures foretold,

For them all to share widely his good news,*Lk 24:45*

Disciples now seen firsthand, not trusting,*Lk 24:48*

So go faithfully forth, the Son then said,*Jn 20:21*

But tarry first for Spirit of Father,

His power come down in Jerusalem,*Lk 24:49*

Son breathing on them, imparting Spirit,*Jn 20:22*

That they now decide others get good news,*Jn 20:23*

As God breathed life into Adam's nostrils,*Gen 2:7*

Making of Adam a living being,

Moses and Aaron crying out facedown

That God 'lone gives breath to all living things,*Num 16:22*

Remembering, O God, our lives but breath,*Job 7:7*

In your hand, is the breath of all mankind,*Job 12:10*

Your breath alone giving understanding,*Job 32:8*

Lowborn but breath, highborn but lie,*Psa 62:9*

Breath taken dead,*Psa 104:29* days like fleeting shadows,*Psa 144:4*

So that every breath would praise the Lord.*Psa 150:6*

Doubting disciple Thomas joined, missing

Son, insisting disbelief unless he

Put fingers in nail wounds, hands in Son's side,*Jn 20:24*

Week later, when Son 'gain came through locked doors,*Jn 20:26*

Thomas did so, crying out the Son was all,

Son saying better believe without seen.*Jn 20:27*

Praying won't work without believing him,*Jas 1:6*

Doubters getting nothing from the Father, *Jas 1:7*

Unstable in ev'rything,*Jas 1:8* God obv'ous,*Ro 1:19*

His qualities known from his creation,*Ro 1:20*

So use mind and eyes to know the Father,*Ro 1:21*

And stop condemning yourself with your doubts;*Ro 14:23*

Snatch doubters from the fire,*Jude 22* Son already

Having appeared to hundreds of others,*Jn 20:24*

And win special favor for faith unseen,*Jn 20:27*

Rather than demand encore appearance.

The Son appeared 'gain by Galilee's sea,

When disciples had wasted night fishing,*Jn 21:1*

Son standing ashore, calling boat, throw net

On other side, bemusing disciples,

Who, astounded, pulled in so many fish

    Boat could not hold,_Jn 21:4_ then recognizing Lord,

Beach figure was Son, Peter fully clad

    Jumped in the water, thrashing for shore,_Jn 21:7_

Where the Son already had fish fire,

    Bread cooked, one more meal to eat with their Lord._Jn 21:9_

You'll die if you don't rely on the Son,_Jn 8:21_

    Admitting Son came from Father, or done,_Jn 8:24_

Your body without Spirit no good form,_Ro 7:5_

    Living for your body useless in death,_Ro 7:6_

Living for the body, sure then to die,_Ro 8:12_

    Caring nothing for spirit, bury dead._Matt 8:21_

Disciples ate with resurrected Son

    Who thrice asked Peter if he loved the Son,

Peter replying that the Son so knew,_Jn 21:15_

    Son telling Peter to care for his sheep,_Jn 21:15_

That when Peter old, others would hands stretch,

    Death, tradition upside down, on a cross,_Jn 21:17_

Son saying nonetheless to follow him,_Jn 21:19_

    Though beloved John may remain for return._Jn 21:20_

The Son's death gave Father back all he made,_Col 1:20_

    Son's sure reward to rejoin his Father,_Heb 12:2_

Father giving you his Son for your all,_Ro 8:32_

    Freeing you from self's certain slavery,_Ro 6:6-7_

Living now for him rather than yourself,_2Co 5:15_

    Son dying prisoner to make you free,_Heb 13:12_

Caring not for world, but for life to come,*Heb 13:14*

    Straight to the Father as the Son first went,*Heb 10:19*

No longer any reason to fear death,*Heb 2:15*

    Needing only deny self, follow him.*Mk 8:34*

Love old life, lose new; hate old, 'ternal new,*Jn 12:25*

    World nothing, only Son winning your soul.*Lk 9:25*

Witnesses

Hundreds others witnessed the risen Son,

    More than five-hundred witnesses at once,*1Co 15:5*

Appeared also to his half-brother James,

    Last to abnorm'lly born apostle Paul,*1Co 15:7*

Peter telling Jerusalem's Pent'cost

    Crowd they all witnessed resurrected Son,*Acts 2:32*

So proclaimed openly, many would see,*Acts 10:40*

    Apostles choosing Matthias among

Many apostle cand'dates who saw Son,

    To replace the dead betrayer Judas.*Acts 1:21*

The Son rose on the third day as foretold,*1Co 15:3*

    Foreshadowed when Pharaoh drew cupbearer

From three days' prison dark, restored 'side throne,*Gen 40:13*

    Moses' outstetched hand plunged Egypt into

Three days' dark, while his people lived in light,*Exo 10:22*

    Joshua waited three days Jordan to cross,

To take Israel into God's promised land,*Joshua 1:11*

    Jonah was in whale's belly three days and

Nights before spit living mission ashore,*Jonah 1:17*

    By Father's tremendous strength, new life won,*Eph 1:19*

Son now controlling both living and dead,*Ro 14:9*

    Father making Son first of many more.*1Co 15:20*

If the Son is dead, then faith is useless;*1Co 15:14*

    If no one comes back to life, then forget it.*1Co 15:16*

Pity if faith is only good this life,*1Co 15:19*

    But Father gave Son new life, many more,*1Co 15:20*

Father to rule the living, not the dead,*Mk 12:26*

    Son coming not to condemn but rescue.*Jn 12:47*

The Lord had looked for justice and seen none,

    Displeased, appalled that no one intervened,*Isa 59:15*

And so his Son worked salvation for him,

    His own righteousness justice sustained,*Isa 59:16*

So that although darkness covers the earth,

    Nations come to his light, to his bright dawn.*Isa 60:2*

Ascension

The Son many times told his disciples

    He would ascend to rejoin his Father,*Jn 6:60*

Said plainly he was going to Father,*Jn 14:12*

    Preparing them for no apparition,*Jn 14:28*

Returned for their good, better he do so,*Jn 16:5*

    As he told Magdalene who feet clasped,*Jn 20:17*

As Elijah ascended in whirlwind,

    Surrounded by fire chariot and horses,*2Kings 2:11*

Jacob dreamed of heaven's staircase, angels

    Ascending and descending, at Bethel,*Gen 28:12*

Micah prophesied that the One, their King,

    Would break open, the way up before them.*Micah 2:13*

Disciples went to Galilean mount,

    Meeting and honoring the Son again,*Matt 28:16*

Ready to witness the Father's power,

    Your power now, too, with Son back to life,*Eph 1:19*

All not yet restored,*2Ti 2:18* some way still to go,

    Pressing toward your incomparable goal,*Php 3:12*

Your dead body into celestial form,*Php 3:20*

    Alive to follow Son, gain all to die,*Php 1:20*

Hard then whether live or die, living for

    Others, dying better to be with Son.*Php 1:22*

'Fore ascension, the Son commissioned his

    Followers with all his authority,

Disciples to reach all with the good news,

    Baptizing into Father, Son, and Spirit,

Teaching others, knowing Son was with them,*Matt 28:18*

    Then lifting hands, saying he cared for them,

The Son rose upward 'til out of their sight,*Lk 24:50*

    Father hiding Son in cloud as did so,*Acts 1:9*

Spectacular,*1Ti 3:16* disciples looking up

    Intently, 'til two in white sudd'nly stood,

Asking why look up when Son would return

    In same wondrous manner as ascension.*Acts 1:10*

Disciples returned to Jerusalem,

Rejoicing,*Lk 24:53* many more so amazed they

Joined in following the Son,*Eph 4:8* ascension

Greatest ever happened to one on earth.*Eph 4:9*

The Son said to be glad he ascended

Because his Father is greater than he,*Jn 14:28*

Although you belong to him either way,*Ro 14:7*

All dying until all could live in Son,*1Co 15:22*

So rather than believe in nothing,

Believe true things, witnessed, verified, sure.*Acts 23:8*

Alighting

Father and Son sent Spirit as promised,

Disciples together for Pentecost,

Waiting as the Lord instructed, praying,

When a great roar of wind filled their building,*Acts 2:1*

Like the great wind God sent to dry the earth

Of Noah's flood, restoring nat'ral life,*Gen 8:1*

Great wind that carried Egypt's ravenous

Locusts into the Red Sea, leaving none,*Gen 10:19*

Night-long wind that divided waters for

Dry land Israel 'fore Pharaoh's army cross,*Gen 14:21*

Lord's wind that drove sea-quail food cubits deep,*Num 11:31*

Wind on which the Lord came down to save.*2Sam 22:11*

Tongues of fire seeming to descend, sep'rate,

Alight on each, Spirit filled, to tongues speak.*Acts 2:3*

A bewildered festival crowd gathered,

Foreigners from many nations, each whom

Heard the tongues in their own foreign language,*Acts 2:5*

    Amazed at Spirit's gift, wondering what

Signs meant, although some made fun they were drunk,*Acts 2:7*

    As you once indulged appetites, to die,

But now you live in the Spirit's new way,*Ro 7:6*

    Thinking of what the Spirit desires,*Ro 8:5*

Fleeing corrupting desires of youth,*2Ti 2:22*

    Not getting drunk, which only corrupts you,*Eph 5:18*

Appetites killing the mind, while Spirit

    Gives your mind the Father's full life and peace.*Ro 8:6*

Peter declared that none were drunk, being

    Nine in the morning, 'stead foretold Spirit

Had come to rescue ev'ryone in Son,*Acts 2:14*

    All present having seen the risen Son,

Knowing Father power Spirit to send,

    Whom they had all just heard and seen descend,*Acts 2:32*

Now appalled that they had killed God's Son,

    Heartbroken, asked what they could poss'bly do,

Reassured need only turn to the Son,

    Immersed, trusting also in his rescue,*Acts 2:36*

Peter's warning effective, baptizing

    Thousands that day, many more following.*Acts 2:39*

The Spirit cleans you up for your rescue,*2Th 2:13*

    Not all, but those who accept the good news,*Ro 15:16*

So know you are the Spirit's container,*1Co 6:19*

    Better Spirit rescue than law condemn you,*2Co 3:8*

Spirit saying to listen to his voice,*Heb 3:7*

> Right things now in mind,*Heb 10:16* works mysterious,*1Ti 3:16*

Complete when happy doing your good works,*Ro 14:17*

> Spirit led, your only way to Father.*Mk 3:29*

Empowering

Spirit more than 'lighted but empowered,

> Peter when seized and jailed for questioning,

No more shirked but proclaimed priests had killed Son

> Whom Father swift brought back for ev'ryone.*Acts 4:8*

Likewise, when priests jailed, threatened, and released

> Peter and John, they prayed that the Father

Have them speak with even greater boldness,

> Power shaking place as Spirit filled them,*Acts 4:22*

As when Jeremiah hesitated

> To speak,*Jer 1:6* the Lord reached out to touch his mouth,*Jer 1:9*

Disciples devoted to common work,*Acts 2:42*

> Staying together, sharing all they had,*Acts 2:44*

Continuing to meet and eat as one,

> Happily honoring Father in peace.*Acts 2:46*

Fine to forego food, not for attention,

> For focus on Father,*Matt 6:16* but look eating,

So only Father notices, rewards,*Matt 6:17*

> As disciples fast with the Son away.*Lk 5:33*

Fasting is hard, so don't make it harder,*Matt 9:16*

> Not to justify,*Lk 18:9* but prepare you,*Acts 13:1* and

To commit leaders to the Father's work,_{Acts 14:23}

Fasting and praying to draw near Father.

Peter and others confronted Council,

Saying God gives Spirit to who obey,_{Acts 5:32}

As to Stephen for wonders and wisdom,_{Acts 6:8}

Philip to lead many to baptism,_{Acts 8:14}

A Roman commander and those with him,

When Peter shared with them the Son's good news,_{Acts 10:36}

Spirit descending across the region,

Though not for Simon sorcerer's money._{Acts 8:18}

The Spirit shares reality, truth, as

The Father sees and speaks it, and makes plans,_{Jn 16:13}

So rely on the Spirit, the Son taught,_{Acts 1:2}

Who helps you and others do as God says;_{Ro 15:18}

Forget your made-up stuff for Spirit's real,_{1Co 2:13}

Spirit showing God's way sound, not foolish,_{1Co 2:14}

Spirit helping you see as the Son sees,_{1Co 2:15}

Spirit making you not just smart but wise,_{Col 1:9}

Spirit directing you to what matters,_{1Pe 1:12}

Transforming you forever, for better._{1Th 1:5}

The Spirit transformed the apostle Paul,

Who persecuted the Son's followers,

'Til blinding light flashed, and Son rebuked Paul,_{Acts 9:1}

Sending him to Damascus where he met

Ananias who vision showed,_{Acts 9:10} to

Restore Paul's sight for good news to Gentiles,_{Acts 9:15}

Placing hands on Paul to receive Spirit_{Acts 9:17}

162

Accept baptism, rely on the Son,*Acts 9:18*

And share the good news, astonishing all,*Acts 9:20*

Former persecutor, fearless witness.*Acts 9:27*

Others whom persecution scattered shared

The good news, many turning to the Son,*Acts 11:19*

Paul, full of Spirit, teaching great numbers,*Acts 11:22*

Going to Gentiles when Jews rejected,*Acts 13:46*

The Spirit giving Paul wonder powers

Like Peter and John had, to share good news,*Acts 13:2*

Spirit on some in tongues and prophesy,*Acts 19:1*

Like Eldad and Medad prophesying

In the desert-wandering Jews' camp,*Num 11:26* yet

Paul obeying despite prison hardships.*Acts 20:22*

Spirit gives diff'rent gifts*1Co 12:4* for common good,*1Co 12:7*

Wisdom, knowledge, faith, healing, miracles

Prophesy, insight, interpretation,*1Co 12:8*

Spirit deciding who gets which good gift,*1Co 12:11*

Before you even think of what you need,*Ro 8:26*

Bringing you love, joy, peace, patience, kindness,

Goodness, faithfulness, gentleness, control,*Gal 5:22*

Making you alive,*Gal 5:25* strong, loving, and stable,*2Ti 1:7*

Living in you, showing what to believe,*2Ti 1:13*

Overflowing hope from Spirit's power,*Ro 15:13*

Filling you until you sing to others,*Eph 5:18*

Moving as freely as the wind blows you.*Jn 3:8*

In the Spirit's power, Peter instantly

Healed a man's legs so he could walk and jump,*Acts 3:1*

Healed bedridden man to get up and walk,*Acts 9:32*

    People bringing their sick into the streets

For Peter's passing shadow to heal them,*Acts 5:12*

    Many coming to Son's rescue result,*Acts 9:35*

Philip healed many paralyzed and lame,*Acts 8:5*

    As did Paul, telling a man lame from birth

To stand, at which the man jumped up to walk,*Acts 14:8*

    Cloth that touched Paul alone curing the sick,*Acts 19:11*

Paul healing a chief official's father

    And the rest of the sick on whole island.*Acts 28:7*

Persecution

Apostle John had vision how good news

    Would spread quickly through Son's body the church,*Rev 12:1*

How beautiful she to her darling Lord,*Song 1:15*

    Like a lily among young-women thorns,*Song 2:2*

Great oppressor trying to destroy all

    Who heard and accepted the Son's good news,*Rev 12:4*

Followers in flight spread the good word,*Rev 12:5*

    Father having settled the sure outcome,

Satan fighting only for earthly time,*Rev 12:7*

    'Til Son's sacrifice permanent defeat,*Rev 12:10*

But meantime filling earth with his fury,*Rev 12:12*

    Persecuting church, awaiting return.*Rev 12:13*

The Son foretold his disciple's wide flight,*Matt 10:22*

    Persecutors condemning them to death,*Matt 24:9*

Priests jailing and questioning Peter and John,*Acts 4:1*

    Jailing again, angel freeing them to

Declare the good news in Temple courtyards,*Acts 5:17*

    Ordered again not to preach but refused,

Until nearly martyred but flogged instead,*Acts 5:25*

    Peter imprisoned for angel to release,*Acts 12:3*

Priests conspiring also to martyr Paul,*Acts 9:23*

    Who several times faced down his own death.

When persecution comes, let the Spirit

    Tell you what to say and how to say it.*Matt 10:19*

The Father lets those who reject the Son

    Go crazy, corrupt, and cursed;*Ro 1:28* weep for them.*Ro 9:2*

Wherever the disciples went, they faced

    Severe persecution, crowd stoning Paul,*Acts 14:19*

Officials flogging Paul and Silas for

    Rebuking a spirit out of a slave,*Acts 16:19*

Synagogue leaders seizing Paul to kill,*Acts 21:27*

    But the good news nonetheless spread widely.

Many converted when Peter raised the dead,*Acts 9:42*

    Others when Paul blinded an opponent,*Acts 13:6*

Father opening hearts of whole households,*Acts 16:13*

    E'en jailer's fam'ly when angel freed Paul,*Acts 16:25*

Even in Athens, Paul spurring to faith,*Acts 17:22*

    Opposition drawing them attention.*Acts 18:5*

So don't fear your persecutors;*Matt 10:26* stand firm

    Because you'll get your rescue when you do.*Lk 21:12*

Expect hardship before your welcome rest,*Acts 14:22*

While you keep on speaking the Son's good news,*Acts 18:9*

Serving humbly, even if with hard tears,*Acts 20:19*

Considering present life worth nothing,*Acts 20:23*

Being ready bound and to die for Son,*Acts 21:13*

Always acting worthy of the good news,*Php 1:27*

Not complaining of hardships like wand'ring

Jews among whom the Lord's angry fire burned,*Num 11:1* or

Jonah when worm ate the Lord's leafy plant,*Jonah 4:6*

Letting sun blaze on the prophet's head,*Jonah 4:8* but

Delighting in persecutions for Son,*2Co 12:10*

Blessing those who curse you, while enduring,*1Co 4:12*

Showing Father saves you but destroys them,*Php 1:28*

Though you face fear within, conflicts outside,*2Co 7:5*

Asking God to defeat persecution,*2Co 1:11*

While standing firm for your own salvation.*Mk 13:13*

As Jeremiah prayed, God to avenge

Persecutors,*Jer 15:15* putting them to their shame,*Jer 17:18*

The Lord, a mighty warrior, be with you,*Jer 20:11*

Cursing those who hate and persecute you.*Deut 30:7*

Martyrs

Opponents martyred many disciples,

Conspiracy bound by oath to kill Paul,*Acts 23:12*

Making false trial charges against him,*Acts 25:1*

Binding Paul o'er to testify in Rome,*Acts 23:9*

Where Paul would win his long-sought martyrdom,

Disciples scum, garbage in the world's eyes,*1Co 4:13*

On display, condemned to die, for good news,*1Co 4:9*

Spectacle to ev'ryone, ev'rywhere,*1Co 4:9*

Appearing fools for the Son, others wise,*1Co 4:10*

Hungry, thirsty, in rags, brut'lly treated,

Homeless, but working hard with their own hands,*1Co 4:11*

Imprisoned, flogged severely, death exposed.*2Co 11:24*

You carry God's good news in weak body,

Showing God's power, not your own power,*2Co 4:7*

Looking like it's over for you, when not,*2Co 4:8*

Death threatening, for you to show Son's life,*2Co 4:10*

Looking like you're losing when you're winning,*2Co 4:16*

Your little trouble now earning reward,*2Co 4:17*

Happy about your weakness, rejoicing,

Seeming weak when you are actually strong.*2Co 12:10*

Synagogue of Freedmen members stirred false

Witnesses against Stephen,*Acts 6:8* who quiet

Remained, looking completely innocent,*Acts 6:12*

Until giving his accusers hist'ry

Lesson in their stubbornness, murdering

Wonderful Son while disobeying law,*Acts 7:1*

Like Aaron's sons Nadab and Abihu,

Offering unauthorized fire 'fore Lord,*Lev 10:1*

Stephen seeing sky open to the Son,*Acts 7:54*

While infuriated leaders stoned him.*Acts 7:57*

Great persecution then broke out 'gainst church,

Scattering all but a few disciples,*Acts 8:1-3*

Priests imprisoning the Son's followers,*Acts 9:1*

    John's brother James killed,*Acts 12:1* Antipas, also.*Rev 2:13*

All will soon hate you because of the Son,*Mk 13:13*

    Though worldly people hate the Son first;*Jn 15:18*

If you act worldly, then they won't hate,*Jn 15:19*

    But persecuting Son, they must you, too,*Jn 15:20*

Yet just getting you the Father's favor,*Matt 5:10*

    When they insult you because of the Son.*Lk 6:22*

So be glad for persecution's reward,*Matt 5:12*

    Relying wholeheartedly on the Son.*Php 1:13*

Persecution can feel like death sentence,

    But makes you rely more on the Father.*2Co 1:9*

While some intensely persecute the church,*Gal 1:13*

    Those same may soon preach the good news, like Paul.*Gal 1:23*

The Father forgives even violent

    Persecutors who act in ignorance.*1Ti 1:13*

Outsiders

The Son's rescue was for everyone,

    Both Jews and Gentiles, as events soon showed.

A devout centurion Cornelius had

    Angelic vision to send for Peter,*Acts 10:1*

Who trance befell about freedom from rules,*Acts 10:9*

    Explaining to Cornelius that all were

Now clean, Jews and Gentiles, under the Son,*Acts 10:26*

    Father showing no favoritism but

168

Accepting people of all nations when they

    Fear him and do right,*Acts 10:34* in the Son's good news,*Acts 10:36*

For Israel was once Canaan foreigner,*Exo 6:4*

    Foreigner Egypt, too, not to oppress,*Exo 23:9*

Law requiring equal with native born;*Lev 19:34*

    God owns all land, making foreigners all,*Lev 25:23*

Strangers in his sight, your days like shadow,*1Chron 29:15*

    Yet foreigners embraced for loving him,*Isa 56:6*

Allotted part Israel's inheritance,*Ezek 47:22*

    For residing among Father's chosen,

Inheritance promised Zelophehad

    Who wilderness died, daughters inherit.*Num 27:7*

As Cornelius sought Peter, so appoint

    Sound church leaders who rely on the Son,*Acts 14:23*

Humble, patient, temp'rate, gentle, honest,*Tit 1:7*

    Not like Moses Egyptian beater kill,

Flee Midian wilds marry priests daughter,*Exo 2:15* but

    Hospitable, self-controlled, who love good,*Tit 1:8*

Don't order around, 'stead 'ppealing gently,*Phm 8-9*

    And who adhere gladly to the good news.*Tit 1:9*

Follow their instruction,*Acts 16:1* in keeping order,*Tit 1:6*

    And in leading their own family well.*1Ti 3:4*

Spirit came on Gentiles who heard Peter,

    Whom they baptized in the Son like the Jews.*Acts 10:44*

Jews criticized Peter who explained that

    The Spirit accepted the Gentiles, too.*Acts 11:1-18*

So whether first or last, inside or out,

Don't think much of yourself, staying sober,*Ro 12:3*

Testing your own actions, doing your best

Without comparing yourself to others,*Gal 6:3*

No pride or conceit, friends with others,*Ro 12:16*

Putting the Father well above yourself,*1Pe 5:6*

Serving the Father with great humil'ty,

Even tears over your inad'quacy.*Acts 20:19*

Book 10: Return

Recovery

Though Son ascended, he soon-King returns,

    Both to recover and restore all his,*2Pe 3:9*

That lion would lie down with lamb, little

    Child leading, no harm on holy mountain,*Isa 11:6*

As God shut mouths of lions in the den

    Into which King Darius threw Daniel,*Dan 6:22*

In but little while, not taking too long,*Heb 10:37*

    Descending as he ascended, with loud

Archangel command, blast of God's trumpet,

    Dead in Christ rising from temp'rary graves,*1Th 4:16*

Living in Christ rising with them in cloud

    To meet Lord in air, fore'er together,*1Th 4:17*

All you've long awaited,*1Th 5:4* God opening

    Sky showing blazing Son, angels surround,*2Th 1:7*

Promised return, assured reward, all new,*2Pe 3:13*

    Second coming, first return, full rescue.*Heb 9:27*

You are in Father's fam'ly forever,*Jn 8:34*

To see Father's face,*Matt 18:10* no children to die,*Matt 18:14*

    Son bringing you to Father, 'nother child,*Heb 2:13*

      Son's sure sibling, all the same family.*Heb 2:12*

The Spirit confirms you as Father's child,*Ro 8:16*

      Your faith in the Son your birth certif'cate.*Gal 3:26*

The Son opens your way to paradise,

      For none but those who enter through the Son,*Jn 3:13*

Where you'll see angels coming and going,*Jn 1:50*

      The Father's place the Son opened for you.*Heb 9:24*

When Son returns, Father's glory, angels

      Galore, Son rejects those rejecting him,*Mk 8:38*

But makes you like him, seeing him as is,*1Jn 3:2*

      Father still molding you for that return,*Php 1:6*

When you'll be ready for him, like he is,*Col 3:4*

      If you keep doing as he says to do,*1Th 3:13*

Evil then over for good, forever,*2Th 2:7*

      Son first, then all those who belong to him.*1Co 15:23*

Because his return exposes your all,

      Better you live right now, Son coming soon,*2Pe 3:11*

Like the East's greatest man Job lived, blameless,

      Upright, fearing God, and shunning evil.*Job 1:3*

Stand for Christ now, when doing so still counts,*Mk 8:38*

      Because things will be hard for those who don't.*2Th 1:8*

Do ev'rything right now, as you 'wait end,*2Pe 3:14*

      Given warning, long gain, not short-term fun,*2Pe 3:17*

Smart about what you know, wise you don't know,*Php 1:9*

      No reason, return, to leave you behind.*1Th 3:13*

Fulfillment

You wait for the Son's certain soon return,*Rev 1:1*

    Like John, writing and sharing widely what's

Coming, so that fewer fail to prepare,*Rev 1:9*

    Seeing Christ's return coming from long off,*Eph 1:8*

Having decided to share Son's return,*2Pe 3:13*

    Those you invited making good for you,*1Th 2:20*

Son's return for them, party's sure part, too,*1Th 4:18*

    Crowned heads all, each celebrant wanting it,*2Ti 4:8*

Multitudes, multitudes! in decision's

    Valley, with the day of the Lord so near,*Joel 3:14*

Knowing God not lie like man, but fulfills,*Num 23:19*

    Ev'ry promise, as Joshua declared,*Joshua 23:14*

As servant Abigail knew God would do

    For her lord David, he still unavenged,*1Sam 25:30*

Fulfilled for Solomon, promised David,*1Kings 8:24*

    Satisfied Jehu to fourth gen'ration.*2Kings 15:12*

The Son returns when all good news have heard,

    None left behind unless so desiring,*Matt 24:14*

Come celestial crowd, unchallenged takover,*Matt 25:31*

    None avoiding, that day coming for all.*Lk 21:35*

Condemn none, lest you also face judgment,*Matt 7:1*

    Condemn none, then you too face no judgment.*Lk 6:37*

You must meet the same measure that you use;*Matt 7:2*

    Fix your big problems before others' small,*Lk 6:41*

Yours sin first, only then helping others,*Matt 7:5*

> Judging correctly from within not out.*Jn 7:24*

Only perfect Son can condemn others;*Jn 8:7*

> You condemn self when doing the same things,*Ro 2:1*

Judging others what you do, judging you,*Ro 2:2*

> So let God accept who know less than you,*Ro 14:2*

Others serving God and not serving you,

> So no bus'ness judging them, God will do.*Ro 14:4*

Others who diminish your service pay,*1Th 2:16*

> But let God set their debt for it, not you,*Ro 12:17*

Avoiding revenge, God handling it best,*Ro 12:19*

> You do opposite, killing with kindness,*Ro 12:20*

Not Samson, setting Philistine standing

> Grain ablaze with twin-tied foxes' tails,*Jdg 15:4* and

Not Haman's pole to impale Mordecai,*Esther 5:14*

> Who turned Xerxes against him,*Esther 7:9* but rather

Overcoming wrong with right,*Ro 12:21* two wrongs less,*1Th 5:15*

> Enduring others, Father endures you,*Col 3:13*

As David let Shimei rain down curses

> And stones, letting the Lord alone avenge,*2Sam 16:13*

Setting your enduring face like flint that

> You not suffer disgrace or be ashamed.*Isa 50:7*

Succession

> The Father orders, divine plan perfect,

> > The Son first returning to gather his,*1Co 15:23*

Then Son assuming all authority,

Ev'rything then come together as been,*1Co 15:24*

Son starting the order, all his control,*1Co 15:25*

Death included, banished for those he saved,*1Co 15:26*

Father giving Son all power, control

Except over Father who all remains,*1Co 15:27*

When Son done, returning all to Father,

Son submitting to Father as should be,*1Co 15:28*

Succession of anointed son to priest

Father role Torah law had so long been,*Lev 6:22*

Eleazar on Aaron's Mos'rah death,*Deut 10:6*

And like prince son succeeds his king father,

Solomon David at Gihon succeed,*1Kings 1:38*

Rehoboam his Solomon succeed.*1Kings 11:43*

Make no mistake: Son has not yet new life

Given to those who died relying him,*2Ti 2:18*

Though Son will sure do so, no grieving you,*1Th 4:13*

Father having promised that those will rise,*1Th 4:15*

When Son returns with all glory fanfare,*1Th 4:16*

Then, your turn, Father drawing you with those,

Together eternally with the Son,*1Th 4:17*

Excited now for Son's coming return.*2Co 1:14*

Encourage others as return approach,*Heb 10:25*

Spectacular celestial appearance,

Reward as you deserve, no more, no less,*Matt 16:27*

Opponents failing in puny power,*Jn 12:48*

Return so soon, Son started and finished,*Rev 22:12*

To recover and restore all things new.*Rev 22:20*

You can make it, praying to the Father,

Escaping awful end to join his Son,*Lk 21:36*

On his return, in his great human train,*Col 3:4*

Trusting his Spirit, celebrating him,*2Th 1:10*

Rejoicing at his side,*1Jn 3:2* looking forward,

Not back to old life to lose ev'rything,*Lk 17:31*

Sober, stable, expecting his return,*1Jn 3:3*

Letting your work ripen into good fruit,*Jas 5:7*

Casting your bread upon the waters that

You may receive your good return for work,*Ecc 11:1*

Father protecting while you wait rescue,*1Pe 1:5*

Staying alert to see Son has for you,*1Pe 1:13*

Father supplying your one lamp-oil need,*1Co 1:7*

As virgins lamps kept waiting their bridegroom,*Matt 25:10*

Ready for banquet, Spirit full, return,*1Co 1:8*

When door shuts on those without Spirit oil.

End

The end has come on the earth's four corners!*Ezek 7:2*

Disaster! See unheard-of disaster!*Ezek 7:5*

Son's return ends all, best end if believe;

But don't let them fool you they are the Son

Or the end has come when it hasn't come,*Mk 13:3*

Conditions so awful the end must near;*Lk 21:9*

Run for the hills in those times when patching

Things up is impossible, worse than e'er.*Matt 24:15*

Armies will surround Jerusalem just

Before its destruction, when you should flee,*Lk 21:20*

The Father keeping it survivable

For those whom the Son saves, others succumb.*Mk 13:20*

Don't believe when people point here and there

At fanciful fakers, fooling the saved;*Matt 24:23*

You'll know the genuine Son, lighting sky*Lk 17:24*

So you can't even see the earth's own sun,*Mk 13:24*

Oceans roaring, some from terror fainting,*Lk 21:25*

Then the Son is come,*Matt 24:32* sky spectacular,*Mk 13:26*

Angels gath'ring all relying on Son,*Matt 24:31*

Looking gladly up when seeing coming,*Lk 21:27*

Those who remembered him before silver

Cord severed, golden bowl broken, pitcher

Shattered at the spring, wheel broken at well,*Ecc 12:6*

Dust returns to ground, spirit God who gave,*Ecc 12:7*

All looking, all seeing, even sorry

Ones who rejected the one saving Son.*Rev 1:7*

The Son judges those who do not trust him,*Jn 8:26*

Who thought were fine on their own without him,*Jn 9:35*

Dividing even family members,*Lk 12:51*

Separating saved one side, not other,*Matt 25:32*

Nothing but long-ago good for those saved,*Matt 25:34*

Who fed hungry, slaked thirst, sheltered homeless,

Clothed naked, healed sick, visited prison,*Matt 25:35*

Doing good to these like doing good him,*Matt 25:37*

But condemning wrongdoers,_{Matt 25:41} who refused

    Help to needy, like refusing him help,_{Matt 25:42}

Thought great time forever, now it's over,_{Matt 25:46}

    Wrongdoers weeping at what is in store._{Lk 13:28}

Timing

Only Father knows when the end will come,_{Matt 24:36}

    Son returning when you least expect him,_{Lk 12:40}

His soon return like Noah's great-flood ark,_{Matt 24:37}

    Catching unaware, going 'bout bus'ness,_{Lk 17:28}

Two working beside, one taken, one not,

    Two in bed, one gone above, other not._{Matt 24:40}

You don't know because Father's time differs,

    Day like thousand years, thousand years like day,_{2Pe 3:8}

Son certain coming back, but God patient,

    None who desire get left behind to die,_{2Pe 3:9}

A time for ev'rything, to live and die,_{Ecc 3:2}

    Tear down and build, mourn and dance, love and hate._{Ecc 3:3}

Last days will rot,_{2Ti 3:1} but Son's return still sneaks up,

    His fire to lay bare, destroy ev'rything,_{2Pe 3:10}

Time nearing, creeping up,_{Php 4:5} see it crouching?_{1Th 1:10}

    Unpredictable but certain to come._{1Th 5:1}

Some mistake that the Son has already come,_{2Th 2:2}

    But the great rebellion must first occur,

Lawless thinking they can do as wanted,

    No matter whom or how many they hurt,_{2Th 2:3}

But don't a lawless evildoer be,

>For the Son has your exquisite rem'dy;_1Ti 6:14_

Just wait for your awful judge, sure and fast,_1Co 4:5_

>Each getting earned, some good, some terror bad._1Co 4:5_

Some fort'nate won't die before they see him,_Matt 16:28_

>But most 'wait his return to judgment rise._Lk 17:22-23_

Not knowing his hour, you must watch for him,_Mk 13:33_

>On lookout, awake, ready, not naked,_Rev 16:15_

Rather, guarding your spiritual redoubt,_Matt 24:43_

>Watch out!_Mk 13:37_ Watch ev'rything, tight ship, on time,_Lk 12:42_

Father putting you in charge if ready,_Matt 24:46_

>Punishing if not care when Son arrives,_Lk 12:45_

Some in right frame of mind, but others not,_Matt 25:1_

>Some jumping to attention,_Matt 25:5-7_ some asleep,_Matt 25:8_

Some promptly joining Son, some left behind,_Matt 25:10_

>Lazy, worthless, thinking God not at work._Matt 25:24-30_

Their silver and gold will not then save them,

>Zephaniah right, God makes sudden end,_Zeph 1:18_

Full force of mis'ry on them in plenty,_Job 20:22_

>Whole disaster for not obeying him,_Jer 44:23_

All curses overtaking for their sin,_Deut 28:15_

>Terrors like flood, tempest snatched at midnight._Job 27:20_

Way

The Son's return is for you, your sole path

>To the Father's whole Son-wrought paradise,_Php 3:13_

179

So look to true destination, not here,*Php 3:20*

 At the Father's great table, ready riches,*Eph 2:6*

Kept there with him so as not to spoil here,*1Pe 1:4*

 Awaiting Son's return, living and dead.*1Th 4:17*

Secure your place in Father's paradise,*2Ti 4:18*

 Dying in the Son to live etern'lly,*2Co 5:1*

Living here briefly, tomorrow unknown,

 So avoid that money-making scheming,*Jas 4:13*

Just doing right, not swearing this or that,*Jas 5:12*

 Never undermining the Son's good news,*Jude 11*

Feeding not just yourself but others, too,*Jude 12*

 Watching out for boasters who flatter you,*Jude 14*

Using your worldly wealth to make good friends,

 So that when gone, you still live forever.*Lk 16:1*

You groan with burden, facing death daily,*2Co 5:4*

 Your reward to enter the Father's house,*Heb 12:28*

Your peril here proving how special there,*2Co 5:2*

 The Father's promised place, perfect new place,*2Pe 3:13*

Expectation feeding your confidence,*Col 1:5*

 In joining the Son beside the Father,*Col 3:1*

Doing all now as in the Father's place,*Matt 18:18*

 Your hope until your end, never released.*Lk 23:42*

The Father judges justly,*Ro 2:5* all laid bare,*Heb 4:13*

 Knowing your secrets,*Ro 2:16* always in the right,*2Th 1:5*

Repaying,*Ro 2:6* avenging reveler wrongs,*1Pe 2:13*

 So satisfy Father, not just others,*1Co 2:15*

Caring little if others judge you but

Sure in your acts not to condemn yourself,*1Co 4:3*

The Spirit guiding you more than conscience

Because the Father judges you; you don't.*1Co 4:4*

The Father uncovers what people hide,

Knowing your true motives, praising the right,*1Co 4:5*

Holding accountable for ev'ry word,

Acquitting or condemning;*Matt 12:36* know the Son.

Power

Apostle John had vision Father's place,

Extr'ordinary revelation sure,

Great voice saying from open heaven door

For John to record what would happen next.*Rev 4:1*

Father sat reg'lly athrone, looking made

Of most precious stones, brilliant colored light

Encircling, twenty-four elders around,*Rev 4:2*

Lightning flashing, thunder pealing from seat,

Spirit fires dancing on crystal sea glass,*Rev 4:5*

Four awesome winged creatures surrounding him,

Chanting endless, phenomenal he'd been,*Rev 4:6*

With each chant elders prostrate fall, giving

Honor and thanks to the Father, making

Ev'rything, including your very being.*Rev 4:9*

Father held sealed scroll, as mighty angel

Asked who could break the seals to read the scroll.*Rev 5:1*

John wept deeply when none appear to read,

'Til elder told John not weep, that Judah's

Lion could open the scroll's seven seals,*Rev 5:3*

    Lamb Son, looking sacrificed, stood at throne,

Adorned with God's seven spirits, took scroll

    From Father's hand, at which awesome creatures

And elders all fell, honoring the Son,*Rev 5:6*

    Singing the Son could open the sealed scroll,

Having died to bring many to worship

    Father, taking over the Son's new earth,*Rev 5:8*

One-hundred-million angels joining song,

    Slain Son now having Father's full honor.*Rev 5:11*

Near the end, scoffers will do evil pleased,

    Saying that the Son is not returning,*2Pe 3:3*

Ignoring Father's plan to end all things,*2Pe 3:5*

    Destroying those who do not follow him,*2Th 1:8*

Saving those good who rely on his Son,*1Pe 2:7*

    None facing judgment until the Son comes.*1Co 4:5*

Rescue

John then had vision, Son opening seals,

    First opened seal spreading judgment 'cross earth,*Rev 6:1*

Second opened seal, evildoers kill,*Rev 6:3*

    Third opened seal, famine came across earth,*Rev 6:5*

Fourth opened seal, death spread around the world,

    Fourth of earth dying from war, plague, famine.*Rev 6:7*

Your rescue immediate, no labor,

The Son's labor having accomplished it.Lk 19:1

Just say you need him, and he rose again;Ro 10:9

Dead men can't rescue, so he must risen,Ro 10:10

Father counts nothing against you, what relief!Col 2:14

Walk with the Son for that welcome relief.1Jn 1:7

John then saw the future spiritual realm,

Son opening fifth seal, Father assured

His dead they had little longer to wait,Rev 6:9

Sixth seal opened, calamity began,

Earth quaking, sun black, moon blood red, meteors

Falling, nature receding, disappeared,Rev 6:12

Living hoping die, Father and Son judging

Evil, unopposed,Rev 6:15 pause for seventh seal,

Angels ensuring one-hundred thousand

First-saved believers would suffer no harm.Rev 7:1

Then John saw many more whom Son had saved,

So many none count, ev'ry nation, joy,Rev 7:9

All angels falling 'fore Father in praise,Rev 7:11

Multitude out world's distracting clamor,

Drawn holy to Son, sacrifice perfect

And brilliant made, like him,Rev 7:13 God protected,

Never hunger, never thirst, never pain,

Son's constant supply, special food, water,

Never tears, ever in his paradise.Rev 7:15

All rising from their graves at his voice, judged

Good to live, evil to condemnation,Jn 5:28

Glorious Father, judging with his Son,Jn 8:50

Dread falling when on the Father's wrong side,*Heb 10:31*

    Anger for self-seekers who reject truth,*Ro 2:8*

Who must Zipporah's intervention seek,

    With flint-knifed foreskin, touch to Moses' feet,*Exo 4:25*

The Father judging fair, fast, and final,*Ro 9:28*

    Kind when doing as he says, stern when not,*Ro 11:22*

Judging everyone, no exceptions,*Ro 14:11*

    Each facing the Father,*Ro 14:12* staying cautious.*1Pe 1:17*

The Father condemns the indulgent lawless,*1Pe 2:10*

    The immoral wicked who hide the truth,*Ro 1:18*

Judging suddenly those sneaking away,*1Th 5:3*

    Father relying on the Son's judgment,*Jn 5:22*

Son's sacrifice judging the world's evil,*Jn 12:30*

    So you may rely on the Savior Son,*Acts 10:42*

For blessed who does not walk with wicked,*Psa 1:1* but

    Meditates day and night on the Lord's law.*Psa 1:2*

Torment

John saw Satan give other oppressors

    Power to plague followers of the Son,*Rev 13:1*

Beast mimicking the Son's resurrection

    So people fear false power, honoring

Beast rather than Son,*Rev 13:3* beast slandering Son,*Rev 13:5*

    Casting aside Father's people so all

Honor beast, 'cept ones relying on Son,

    Beast capturing and killing followers.*Rev 13:7*

Torment will worsen under a second beast,

    Like the first beast, swaying non-believers,_{Rev 13:11}

Doing things looking like wonders but false,

    Fooling those who do not follow the Son,

Killing who refuse to worship image,_{Rev 13:13}

    Forcing all to receive beast's mark,

Without which they can neither buy nor sell,_{Rev 13:16}

    Beast's number man's number, just six, six, six._{Rev 13:18}

Judgment

The Lamb opened seventh and final seal,

    Seven angels trumpets ready, 'nother

Angel hurling earth's judgment in thunder

    And lightning, shaking the earth's foundation._{Rev 8:1}

With first trumpet blast, hail, fire, and blood fell,

    Destroying one third earth's vegetation;_{Rev 8:7}

With second trumpet blast, a huge mountain,

    Ablaze and thrown into the earth's great sea,

Turned the sea into blood, destroying one

    Third of all the sea's creatures and commerce;_{Rev 8:8}

With third trumpet blast, great star Wormwood fell

    Turning water bitter, killing many;_{Rev 8:10}

With fourth trumpet blast, one third of the earth's

    Light went dark, throwing people in despair._{Rev 8:12}

Rejecting the Father draws his judgment;_{Ro 9:17}

    Opposing his teachers angers Father,_{1Th 2:16}

Who reserves the worst for the most corrupt,*1Pe 2:17*

Not sparing his angels who disobeyed,*1Pe 2:4*

Like Gibeah men, who raped visitor's

Concubine,*Jdg 19:25* sent in parts throughout Israel.*Jdg 19:29*

No King seems reign in the hearts of Israel,

Everyone doing as they saw fit,*Jdg 21:25*

Like Queen Vashti refusing king's request

To show her beauty to the people.*Esther 1:12*

John then heard an eagle calling out woe

On earth's inhabitants for three last blasts.*Rev 8:13*

With fifth trumpet blast, star opened Abyss,

Smoke, torturing locusts, covering earth,*Rev 9:1*

Tormenting all but those marked with God's seal,

So they looked for a death they could not find;*Rev 9:4*

Destroyer Apollyon led the torment,*Rev 9:9*

As Satan always seeks to kill, destroy,

Entreating God against most-upright Job,*Job 1:11*

Here ending first woe with two more to come.*Rev 9:12*

Reject Son, die forever, God's anger,*Jn 3:36*

No rescue coming from Father's judgment,*Heb 10:27*

Marked for slaughter unless death's angel see

Sacrificed Son's blood on passover doorframes,*Exo 12:7*

Like 'Zekiel's vision of linen-clothed man

Marking foreheads of followers to spare.*Ezek 9:3*

With sixth trumpet, four Euphrates angels

With two-hundred-million mounted troops killed

One third humankind with fire, smoke, sulfur,*Rev 9:13*

Yet those who survived still did not turn from

Worshipping things they made or from magic,

Murder, and sexual immorality.*Rev 9:20*

Splendorous angel came down from heaven,

Planting feet on sea and land, roaring, while

Holding a small scroll of the Son's good news,*Rev 10:1*

Roar warning seventh blast would accomplish

Father's last myst'ry,*Rev 10:5* of which John to tell,*Rev 10:9*

Church to spread good news 'cross earth, 'gainst awful

Opposition killing followers who

Would live again, ending the second woe.*Rev 11:1*

Seventh blast makes earth Son's 'ternal kingdom,

Elders praising Father for Son's new rule,

Raising the Son's dead, destroying others,

Revealing Father's full promise and plan.*Rev 11:15*

Accept whom the Son sends, honor Son;

Honor the Son, you honor the Father.*Jn 13:20*

Even those far away, looking for else,

Soon seek Son,*Jn 12:20* Father choosing, not your choice,*1Th 1:4*

Father choosing you before you chose him,*Ro 11:1*

But still pursue him,*Ro 11:7* even as he choose,*Ro 11:5*

Knowing you're no better than those ahead,*Ro 11:18*

His chosen ones having worked hard for you,*Ro 11:28*

Rejected at first, so to rescue you,*Ro 11:15*

Then bring all together, truly special.*Ro 11:12*

So stand at the ancient crossroads to look,

Discerning the good way in which to walk,

Then walk in that good way and no other,

    Finding rest for troubled and weary souls.*Jer 6:16*

Father chose despised, e'en made things to choose,*1Co 1:28*

    Inviting all who love him, all for good,*Ro 8:28*

His choice, long before you earned anything,*Ro 9:10*

    Choosing children whom one would not expect,*Ro 9:24*

As if you were special,*Eph 1:4* his first choice,*2Th 2:13* one

    Whom he dearly loves,*Col 3:12* before you were born.

When the Son has gathered his own, they will

    Roar to him a new song only they know,*Rev 14:1*

For Father and Son to celebrate their

    Best of their best, those blameless truthtellers.*Rev 14:4*

Father's first angel will fly to proclaim

    The good news to ev'ry tribe and nation,

Saying fear and worship creator God,*Rev 14:6*

    With the hour of his last judgment now come.*Rev 14:7*

Father's second angel follows, saying

    Corrupt Babylon had fin'lly fallen.*Rev 14:8*

Third angel cries those taking beast's mark face

    God's wrath, torment before Son and angels,*Rev 14:9*

While God's own endure patiently 'waiting

    Their rest and reward for fruitful labors,*Rev 14:12*

As Xerxes rewarded Esther with crown

    In place of disobedient Vashti.*Esther 2:17*

Gold-crowned Son of Man then harvests the earth

    Of wrongdoers,*Rev 14:14* angel aided, trampling

Harvest so blood rivers flow in fury,*Rev 14:17*

As Father in Noah's day rid the earth,*1Pe 2:5*

Burned Sodom and Gomorrah to the ground,*Gen 19:24*

Destroying lawless who pretend to rule,*2Th 2:3*

Those who, rejecting God, know not doing,*1Pe 2:12*

Teaching one another their hard lessons,*Matt 12:41*

Worldly evil, now over, done, condemned,*Jn 16:8*

Given over to endless perversion,*Jude 5*

Fit only for hell, chained for last judgment,*1Pe 2:4*

Whom angels separate for destruction.*Matt 13:47*

Fury

John then saw vision of seven angels,

Seven last plagues showing Father's anger.*Rev 15:1*

Followers who had defeated the beasts

Stood beside sea of fire, playing Father's

Instruments,*Rev 15:2* singing Moses and Jesus,

Leading their people out of slavery,*Rev 15:2*

Christ beautiful, glorious, servant Branch,*Zech 3:8*

Pride of rescued survivors in Israel,*Isa 4:2*

Angels brought out seven plagues*Rev 15:5* and seven

Golden bowls filled with the Father's fury.*Rev 15:7*

God plays no favorites,*Ro 2:11* treating alike,*Ro 2:8*

Father of all, rewarding pursuers,*Ro 10:12*

Choosing the poor to love him, get reward,*Jas 2:5*

Watching you without partiality,*1Ti 5:21*

Like David bringing from poor Lo Debar, lame

Mephibosheth, to eat at king's table.*2Sam 9:6*

Angels poured first bowl, leaving festering

Sores on those with beast's mark, honoring him,

Second bowl pouring blood, killing the sea,

Third bowl pouring blood judgments on waters,*Rev 16:2*

Fourth bowl making sun scorch cursed people,*Rev 16:8*

Fifth bowl plunging beast's rule into darkness,*Rev 16:10*

Sixth bowl drying great rivers to nothing,*Rev 16:12*

Beasts then pouring their own awful spirits,*Rev 16:13*

Seventh bowl bringing loud voice saying o'er,*Rev 16:17*

Earthquake collapsing all the earth's cities,*Rev 16:18*

Natural features disappearing, while

Hundred-pound hailstones fell on the people.*Rev 16:18*

God sure shares visions and revelations,*2Co 12:1*

Things that others cannot even express.*2Co 12:4*

Listen to the Father's warnings,*Heb 12:25* beyond

The simple stuff,*Heb 6:1* reaching maturity,*Heb 6:3*

No longer thinking like children,*1Co 14:20* grown up,*1Pe 2:2*

Learning spiritual, not just material.*Jn 3:10*

Angel told John he saw end not only

Of Satan but also false religion,

Aligned with world rather than the Father,*Rev 17:1*

Glittering while obviously still carnal,*Rev 17:3*

Destroying many close Son followers,*Rev 17:5*

Satan rallying last lost ones,*Rev 17:7* soon to

Perish,*Rev 17:9* after one last warring 'gainst Son,

Who will quickly win his own followers,*Rev 17:12*

Multitudes from ev'ry people, nation,*Rev 17:15*

Leaving Satan turned inward, devouring

False religion ruling the earth's leaders,*Rev 17:16*

Until Father accomplishes purpose.*Rev 17:18*

Stay free, as the Father has promised you,*Gal 4:22*

Or desires will hold you for destruction;*Gal 4:24*

No turning to enslaving principles,*Gal 4:9*

Promising freedom but slave to their wrongs.*1Pe 2:19*

No letting your body boss you around,*1Co 9:27*

Offering you nothing but your own death.*Ro 6:21*

When the Son died, enslavement also died,

Making you free forever in the Son.*Ro 6:6*

Victory

John saw angel of great authority

Illuminate the earth with his splendor,

Proclaiming corrupt, truth mixed with falsehood,*Rev 18:1*

Those enjoying excessive luxury,*Rev 18:3*

'Gainst which angel warned, but done anyway,*Rev 18:4*

God returning torment double for that

They once consumed in ill-gained luxury,*Rev 18:6*

Plagues, famine, and death overtaking them,*Rev 18:8*

Earth's wealthy no longer able to enslave,

To make them rich off extrav'gant cargoes.*Rev 18:9*

Thank Father for indescribable gift*2Co 9:15*

That you join him in paradise, heaven,*Heb 12:28*

For the faith of others,*1Th 3:9* for clear conscience,*2Ti 1:3*

    For his word,*1Th 2:13* all he shares with you.*Eph 5:19* in all

Circumstances,*1Th 5:18* for sharing his kingdom,*Col 1:12*

    Singing to the Father in gratitude,*Col 3:16*

Using Spirit-wrought gifts of art, design,

    To worship, as the Lord chose Bezalel*Exo 31:2*

To adorn the tabernacle's sacred

    Furnishings, as the Father's holy place.*Exo 31:11*

Thank Father for faithful brothers, sisters,*2Th 2:13*

    Growing faith and love among followers,*2Th 1:3*

Letting you teach,*1Ti 1:12* instead of old coarse talk,*Eph 5:4*

    Receiving everything with thanksgiving.*1Ti 4:4*

John saw great angel throw boulder in sea,

    Washing away all the earth's corruption.*Rev 18:21*

The Son's multitude of followers roared,

    Honoring the Father for just judgment

Condemning the awful oppressor while

    Fully avenging the Son's followers.*Rev 19:1*

Elders and creatures rejoiced,*Rev 19:4* multitude

    Shouting for Father's reign, rejoicing that

Son had finally joined his followers,*Rev 19:6*

    John told to publish vision, encourage.*Rev 19:9*

John fell at angel's feet, but angel said

    He was mere fellow servant with John and

Others who follow the Son, worshipping

    'Stead Spirit, showing John the Son's vict'ry.*Rev 19:10*

Your suff'ring is so much less than reward,*Ro 8:18*

That you should happily suffer with Son,*1Pe 4:12*

Offenses in Son's name rewarding you,*1Pe 4:14*

Glad others know that you rely on him.*1Pe 4:15*

Father fixing all after you suffer,*1Pe 5:10*

While others also suffer for good news.*2Ti 1:8*

Endure for reward of Son's soon rescue,*2Ti 2:10*

Reigning with Son,*2Ti 2:12* receiving Son's reward.*Lk 22:28*

John saw Son, name only Son knows, the Word,

Wearing many crowns, eyes blazing, blood robe,

Riding white horse,*Rev 19:11* God's armies following,

Soldiers dressed white linen, on white horses.*Rev 19:14*

Son spoke, striking down ev'ry resistance.*Rev 19:15*

Son's robe bore King of kings and Lord of lords.*Rev 19:16*

Angel called scavengers to gather to

Eat flesh of corrupt leaders and people.*Rev 19:17*

Son's army captured beast and false prophet,

Throwing them into burning sulphur while

Killing the beast's army with the Son's words,

Scavengers gorged on oppressor's dead flesh.*Rev 19:19*

Angel locked Satan thousand years Abyss,*Rev 20:1*

After which roam again for a short time.*Rev 20:3*

God then restored Son's dead to enjoy earth,

Satan's dead rising after thousand years*Rev 20:4*

To surround God's people in huge army,*Rev 20:7*

God's fire descending on opposition,

Satan burning in beast's lake forever,*Rev 20:10*

All dead then facing Father's just judgment,*Rev 20:11*

Those not with Son into burning lake with

Satan, beast, death, and even hell itself.*Rev 20:14*

The Son makes his people loving, complete,*1Jn 4:17*

No guilt or fear of Father's punishment,*1Jn 4:18*

Living as you should,*Col 2:10* seeing right and wrong,*Ro 1:17*

Influential and having conviction,*1Th 1:5*

Strong,*1Th 3:8* not succumbing to mess around you,*Gal 1:4*

Perfectly at peace, when others suffer,*2Th 1:8-10*

Receiving Son's own reward, Father's all,*2Th 2:14*

Honoring Father, victor, best of all,*1Ti 1:11*

Knowledge of the Lord's glory filling the

Earth as the waters cover o'er the sea.*Hab 2:14*

New

John saw God's new heaven above, on earth,

Old passed,*Rev 21:1* new Jerusalem descending,

City without walls, so many there dwell,*Zech 2:4*

The Lord its wall of fire, glory within,*Zech 2:5*

Spectacular place for Son and all his,*Rev 21:2*

Father's residence among his people,

With them to honor, obey forever,

Where no tear wells, all sadness kept away,*Rev 21:3*

Death, mourning, crying, pain, absent, away,*Rev 21:4*

Ev'rything new, God's words so commanding,

Reliable, already accomplished,*Rev 21:5*

God beginning and end, start to finish,

Your life source, your victory, you his children,*Rev 21:6*

New peace, new trust, and new stability,

God destroying murderers, immoral,

Those who refuse to honor God and Son.*Rev 21:8*

New heaven is your permanent reward,*1Pe 1:4*

Some already earned for faith in Father,*Ro 4:13*

Poor, rich for Father, receiving reward,*Jas 2:5*

Confident and patient earning reward,*Heb 6:12*

Reward for your least service to the Son's,*Mk 9:41*

God's words building you up for your reward,*Acts 20:32*

Coming not from you but Son's sacrifice,*Heb 9:23*

He only making reward possible,*Heb 9:15*

Angel told John tour Son's new residence,

New Jerusalem descending to earth,*Rev 21:9*

Son foretold,*Rev 3:12* God's glory lighting city,

Angel gates, foundations named disciples,*Rev 21:11*

City fourteen-hundred miles long, wide, high,

Jasper wall two-hundred feet thick,*Rev 21:15* with each

Foundation diff'rent precious stone, each gate

Enormous pearl, streets of transparent gold,*Rev 21:19*

No Temple, constant worship, Father, Son,*Rev 21:22*

Gates always open, no night existing,*Rev 21:25*

Holding all glory, honor,*Rev 21:24* Son approved,*Rev 21:27*

Life's river flowing out throne of God, Lamb,

Like 'Zekiel's vision of water flowing

From Temple in river so vast none cross,*Ezek 47:1*

Down great street, lined fruit trees that feed, heal all,*Rev 22:1*

God and Lamb ruling all, all worship Son.*Rev 22:3*

You need only hold onto the good news,*Heb 10:23*

Father, only your rescue in his mind.*Heb 6:17*

You were not born saved but came to good news,*Eph 2:12*

Together with long-saved and newcomers,*Eph 3:6*

Not to go through motions but to mean it,

To live in God's perfect peace forever,*Heb 4:1*

Swords beaten to plowshares, spears pruning hooks,

Nation not 'gainst nation, nor train for war.*Jonah 4:3*

Eternity

The Son said you live forever with him,*Jn 3:36*

Those who do as he says will never die.*Jn 8:51*

When asked how live forever, Son pointed

To command to love Father with all heart,

Soul, strength, and mind, to love neighbor like self,*Lk 10:25*

Doing as he says, as Father commands.*Jn 12:50*

Believe as you see: immortality;*2Ti 1:10*

Father has honor, glory forever.*1Ti 1:17*

You'd be withered grass or fallen flowers

Without God's everlasting holy word.*1Pe 1:24*

Corruption causes certain death, but Son

Rising back to life ended corruption,

Restoring God's orig'nal perfection,

Letting you live forever, incorrupt.*Ro 5:21*

Immortality is here. You've seen it:

The Father gives new life back after death.*Ro 4:17*

With life back, the Son cannot die again;

Death no longer has its effect on him.*Ro 6:9*

He now lives forever with the Father,*Ro 6:10*

Rising for you so you may rise with him,*1Th 3:10*

Live 'gain when you die relying on him,*2Ti 2:11*

Son having power o'er living and dead.*Ro 14:9*

Son destroyed death for immortality,*2Ti 1:10*

Perishable for imperishable,

Mortal becoming immortal, foretold,*1Co 15:54*

Death losing sting, decay gone, powerless.*1Co 15:55*

People have long trusted Father raise dead,*Heb 11:19*

Faith enabling many die without fear,*Heb 11:37*

So use your mind to see temporary,*2Co 4:18*

But then know eternal,*Heb 1:8* for ev'rything

Disappears, but Father and Son remain,*Heb 1:11*

God unchanging, remaining forever.*Heb 1:12*

Earthly possessions are not eternal,

But Father and Son, they are eternal,*Matt 19:16*

Father loving so much, he let Son die

So you could rely, escape death, live e'er,*Jn 3:16*

No magic potion, but Son relying,*Jn 5:39*

God's plan, Son what he did, you forever.*Jn 17:2*

The Son is truth,*Jn 18:37* just as his wonders showed,*Jn 5:36*

Exactly who and what he said he was.*Jn 5:37*

Spirit now carries Son's truth,*Jn 15:26* you to speak,*Jn 15:27*

Father, Son agreeing, speaking as one,*Jn 8:13*

For can two walk together but they agree?*Amos 3:3*

    A house divided cannot stand 'gainst self.*Mk 3:25*

Scripture records few, Son's endless wonders,

    Enough to know that his good news is true,*Jn 20:30*

None able to record all the Son did,

    For such writings would fill God's universe,*Jn 21:24*

But Spirit repeats what Son said and did,*1Jn 5:6*

    So you choose whether to accept Son's truth:*1Jn 5:10*

The Father gave us eternal life in

    His only Son and only in his Son.*1Jn 5:11*

Destiny

Your destiny: live forever with Son.*Jn 6:40*

    Eat food and die, but eat from Son and live.*Jn 6:50*

Love what you have and lose it, but seek what

    You don't have and gain it, find it, it's yours.*Jn 12:25*

You live joyfully, knowing you live e'er,*2Th 2:16*

    Good as new, forever,*Heb 10:14* Son kept alive.*Jude 20*

Spiritual heroes trusted 'til they died,

    Earth foreign to them,*Heb 11:13* unworthy of them,*Heb 11:38*

Dead before receiving promised reward

    But now made perfect together with you.*Heb 11:39*

Heroes offer the Father better things,*Heb 11:4*

    Abel's consecrating firstborn, firstfruit,

First blood,*Exo 13:2* to honor, worship, serve the Lord,

    Pleasing the jealous Lord so greatly that

Abel did not die but straight ascended,*Heb 11:5*

    As God commends each for their confidence.*Heb 11:2*

Noah's faith had him build ark to save world;*Heb 11:7*

    Isaac's faith assured his children's future;*Heb 11:20*

Jacob's faith assured his grandsons' blessing;*Heb 11:21*

    Joseph's faith predicted slav'ry freedom;*Heb 11:22*

Joshua's trumpet faith fell Jericho's walls;*Heb 11:30*

    Rahab's faith welcomed spies, saving her life.*Heb 11:31*

Other heroes conquered lands, ministered,

    Gained promise, avoided death, and quenched flames,

Each through faithful reliance on Father,

    Weakness becoming strength, routing en'mies.*Heb 11:32*

Share your heroes' faith;*Heb 13:7* shortcuts gain nothing;*Ro 6:21*

    Train to win, not just once but forever.*1Co 9:25*

Living forever is worth trouble now;*2Co 4:17*

    Ask the Son who will give you what you need.*Jn 4:4*

The little you forego now gains fortune,*Mk 10:28*

    So work at it with your life depending;

Son sees your work and gives you what you need,*Jn 6:26*

    So you'll win a paradise life fore'er,*Rev 2:7*

Walking with the Son as your advocate,*Rev 3:4*

    So to Father, you'll be just like his Son.*Rev 3:21*

All will eventually hear the good news,

    So share it,*Mk13:10* letting others know when Son

Does great things for you they'll appreciate,*Mk 5:18*

    Exciting others about the good news,*Lk 16:16*

Serving the good news,*Col 1:23* happy to do so,*1Th 2:7*

Telling the good news to those who don't hear,*1Th 2:16*

Truly working at sharing the good news,*1Th 3:2*

With Son and he with you when you're sharing.*1Jn 4:13*

Father may want you leading in sharing,*Ro 1:1*

So go tell it*Ro 15:19* where others haven't told,

Your fresh work, not relying on others,*Ro 15:20*

Good news from very long ago, always,*Ro 16:25*

Your one duty owed Father who made you

To tell the good news, that others join you.*Ro 15:16*

Don't add to it or take away from it.

Just tell the good news as it always is.*Rev 22:18*

Conclusion

Odd to write and read an epic poem in such secular and distraught day and age as this one, isn't it? Yet each of us have something *epic* about us, the one source of which is the epic One, this righteous Lord Savior Jesus. Without him, we are indeed mundane, trivial, pointless, and hopeless. But with him, we are epic, grand, divine, justified, headed for glory, not the fleeting fame of a tawdry backwater stage, nor the distracting fame of more-decadent Broadway, yes *Broadway* leading to destruction, but weighty glory, permanent glory, the Father's very honor with which he weighted the Son and the Son so lightly and joyously burdens us. Embrace your epic; embrace the Son. Hear the good news, trust the good news, share the good news in full faith and confidence until you receive the Lord's baptism of belief, knowing, not just hoping, that he has destined you for his glory. This good news is epic. Treat it as it is. And may the Lord of glory reign in you from now until... forever.

Abbreviations

Genesis	*Gen*	Nahum	*Nahum*
Exodus	*Ex*	Habbakuk	*Hab*
Leviticus	*Lev*	Zephaniah	*Zeph*
Numbers	*Num*	Haggai	*Haggai*
Deuteronomy	*Deut*	Zechariah	*Zech*
Joshua	*Joshua*	Malachi	*Mal*
Judges	*Jdg*	Matthew	*Matt*
Ruth	*Ruth*	Mark	*Mk*
1 Samuel	*1Sam*	Luke	*Lk*
2 Samuel	*2Sam*	John	*Jn*
1 Kings	*1Kings*	Acts	*Acts*
2 Kings	*2Kings*	Romans	*Ro*
1 Chronicles	*1Chr*	1 Corinthians	*1Co*
2 Chronicles	*2Chr*	2 Corinthians	*2Co*
Ezra	*Ezra*	Galatians	*Gal*
Nehemiah	*Neh*	Ephesians	*Eph*
Esther	*Esther*	Philippians	*Php*
Job	*Job*	Colossians	*Col*
Psalms	*Psa*	1 Thessalonians	*1Th*
Proverbs	*Prov*	2 Thessalonians	*2Th*
Ecclesiastes	*Ecc*	1 Timothy	*1Ti*
Song of Songs	*Song*	2 Timothy	*2Ti*
Isaiah	*Isa*	Titus	*Tit*
Jeremiah	*Jer*	Philemon	*Phm*
Lamentations	*Lam*	Hebrews	*Heb*
Ezekiel	*Ezek*	James	*Jas*
Daniel	*Dan*	1 Peter	*1Pe*
Hosea	*Hosea*	2 Peter	*2Pe*
Joel	*Joel*	1 John	*1Jn*
Amos	*Amos*	2 John	*2Jn*
Obadiah	*Oba*	3 John	*3Jn*
Jonah	*Jonah*	Jude	*Jude*
Micah	*Micah*	Revelation	*Rev*

Other Faith Books by Nelson Miller

Spiritspeak: Sharing Some Very Good News

Gospelspeak: The New Testament

Biblespeak: The Epistles

A Letter to Memphis

The Faithful Lawyer

Answered Prayers

Secret Devotion

Looking to Jesus

Following Jesus

Gospel Stories

Pierce's Cause

Facing Death

CPSIA information can be obtained
at www.ICGtesting.com
Printed in the USA
BVHW041504170119
538098BV00008B/84/P